I0138933

THE RANDOM
LOCAL HISTORY
READER

Fun Stuff for the Inquiring Mind

CUPID IS BAFFLED IN SHEBOYGAN

by The Sheboygan
County Historical
Research Center

978-0-9883759-7-0

Published by the Sheboygan County Historical Research Center
518 Water Street, Sheboygan Falls, WI

schrc.org

All rights reserved.
Published 2014

Introduction

The staff members of the Research Center run across hundreds of really interesting random tidbits of information each year. They need to be shared and appreciated. Great conversation will ensue.

The Random Local History Reader is filled with odd and interesting history. What is the real story of the Dead Horse? Who was the Black Terror of Sheboygan? Have you ever read an obituary for an outhouse? Learn the meaning of the term, Yeggman. Find out why Cupid was baffled. How did Sheboygan celebrate the end of Prohibition. What's up with Elkhart Lake's haunted house. And read the full story behind the murder of revered, early teacher, John Sexton.

Great reading for quiet time or bedtime, you'll enjoy every story and photo included in this random collection of historical gems.

This is an image printed from the first color negative produced in the state of Wisconsin. It was taken by photographer, C.A. Winscher, of Sheboygan. An 8 x 10 glass plate negative, it was produced in 1889, and remains in pristine condition after 125 years.

Crime of a Different Kind

SAFE BLOWERS MAKE RICH HAUL FROM WALDO STATE BANK

Sheboygan Press, October 11, 1917

Safe blowers got into the vault of the Waldo State Bank some time during the night and got about $1,200 worth of stamps, $71 in pennies, wrapped, but missing about $1,800 in cash which had been put in the safe inside. The crooks ruined the vault door as well as the outer safe door, but were unable to penetrate the safe. The stamps were the surplus stock of the post office deposited by Postmaster William Peterson.

What time the robbers invaded the bank could not be determined, although it is believed that it was during the early hours of this morning. David J. Holbrook, assistant cashier of the bank, said he was the last visitor yesterday, entering the bank about 7pm in the evening to fix the fire and use the telephone.

Above: Seen here in 1915, looking south on Depot Street in Waldo, Wisconsin. At left are the Waldo Bank, barber shop, and Dynamite Bill's Tavern.

This morning when he came to the bank at 8 o'clock he found the Yale lock on the outside door removed and immediately sensed something wrong. On stepping inside and looking through the screened partition he saw a yawning hole in the safe door and did not wait to investigate further. . .

Mrs. Ella Wiggin, a nurse attending a patient in the house of Clarence Beeckler, two blocks east, heard an automobile going eastward at high speed at 4 o'clock and J.P. Flanagan, who lives in Cascade, heard one going in the opposite direction about 5 o'clock, either of which, it is believed, might have contained the robbers making their getaway. . . .

One of the effects left by the robbers was soot covering the floor and desks. When Assistant Cashier Holbrook entered the bank he noticed the peculiar smell, but the air seemed clear. It is believed that the men who did the job were well-informed as to the situation. A trio of strangers was in the village a couple of weeks ago. They were three men left here by a coal car. The three were seen washing at the pump at the canning plant. All were smooth faced. One was about 5'4" and stocky and wore dark clothes.

Another one of the three was about 30 years old, weighed about 180 pounds, had a week's growth of beard on his round face. He had an intelligent look. He wore a black suit and checkered shirt and a black Fedora hat.

The third man was about 20 years old, about 5 feet 8 inches high and weighed 130 pounds apparently. His suit and hat were gray. He looked like a fellow addicted to cigarettes. His nose was peaked and his face slim. His coat collar was turned up.

The Waldo robbery was the second bank burglary in Wisconsin this year.

Yeggmen attacked State Bank of Waldo (Sheboygan County) early this morning. Used Acetelyne Gas to open Vault Door. Destroyed outer part of Safe Door (Diebold "Tisco") but failed to secure entrance to Safe and Money.

BANKS ARE URGED TO WATCH FOR YEGGS AND STRANGERS- EXTRA PRECAUTION is necessary on the part of all Banks for next four weeks. Three gangs of Yeggmen recently released from State Prisons are known to be in the section of the country. Ask police to keep a sharp lookout for strangers; a private watchman and a shotgun are worthwhile. (FYI- Yegg is slang for a criminal; esp., a safecracker or burglar) From the Wisconsin Bankers Association.

March 19, 1831 - The first bank robbery in United States history occurs at the City Bank of New York. Edward Smith robbed the Wall Street bank of $245,000. He would be caught and convicted of the crime with sentencing of five years in Sing Sing prison.

Waldo Bank Is Robbed

Two armed bandits robbed the Waldo State Bank of approximately $1,000 in cash at 1:30 p. m. today.

Up to late this afternoon, Sheriff Schmidt reported he had no trace of the bandits.

They walked into the building and held up Chester Harrison, assistant cashier, and Miss Irene Sprangers, clerk, scooping up all the cash that was in sight, and making their getaway in an automobile that was parked in an alley a short distance from the bank.

The men were in the bank approximately ten minutes, one holding up the representatives of the bank and the other guarding the door.

Faces Greased

Neither of the bandits wore a mask, but they both had their faces smeared with grease. They had their blue Chrysler sedan or coupe parked near some sheds between the soft drink parlor of George Gardner (Dynamite Bill) and the bank, off the street.

A. L. Oosterhous, Waldo rural mail carrier entered the bank just as the robbers left. Mr. Harrison and Miss Sprangers still had their hands up.

"We've been robbed," they excitedly informed Mr. Oosterhous when he started in the bank. "Tell 'Chuck'" (Mr. Cross).

Mr. Cross was at the Masonic temple preparing for the banquet of the Sheboygan County Bankers' association which is being held tonight.

Mr. Oosterhous did as he was requested

Mr. Harrison stated that one of the bandits walked inside the cage and ordered him (Mr. Harrison) to open the vault. Mr. Harrison informed the gunman that the vault was locked and that the cashier was out. In this way, he prevented the theft of an additional large quantity of money, as the vault was actually unlocked.

Mr. Cross paid a tribute to the cool-headedness of both Harrison and Miss Sprangers in the presence of the bandits

Headed East—South

Mr. Gardner saw the gunmen running down the street after they left the bank, but he did not become alarmed. He watched them interestedly, thinking they were two young men from the village having a foot race, and it was not until after they had vanished in the Chrysler car that he realized something unusual had happened.

The bandit car went east as far as Onion River, and it is believed they went south from there on Highway 57.

Waldo Bank Robbed Again 1928

EXTRA

Two armed bandits robbed the Waldo State Bank of approximately $1,000 in cash at 1:30pm on Wednesday, July 11, 1928. Sheriff Schmidt reported no trace of the bandits.

They walked into the building and held up Chester Harrison, assistant cashier, and Miss Irene Sprangers, clerk, scooping up all the cash that was in sight, and making their getaway in an automobile that was parked in an alley a short distance from the bank.

The men were in the bank approximately ten minutes, one holding up the representatives of the bank and the other guarding the door.

Neither of the bandits wore a mask, but had their faces smeared with grease. The blue Chrysler sedan was parked near some sheds between the soft drink parlor of George Gardner (Dynamite Bill) and the bank.

A.L. Oosterhous, Waldo rural mail carrier entered the bank just as the robbers left. Mr. Harrison and Miss Sprangers still had their hands up.

Mr. Gardner saw the gunmen running down the street after they left the bank, but he did not become alarmed. He watched them thinking they were two young men from the village having a foot race, and it was not until they vanished in the Chrysler car that he realized something unusual happened.

The car went east as far as Onion River and then probably south on Highway 57.

Hold Black Terror In Jail Here

Latest Chapter Of A "Thrill Program" Is Not So Thrilling — Hold Accomplice

Sheboygan Press—March 12, 1929

Stanley Golichnick, alias "Hickman II," alias Frank Berman, alias John L. Keenan, alias William Norton, Sheboygan's youthful "Black Terror," is in the county jail awaiting circuit court trial.

With him is James Ledden, alleged accomplice whose car the young "terrorist" is reported to have been using in his so-called "thrill" program. Both appeared in municipal court yesterday afternoon and when they waived preliminary hearing, they were bound over to circuit court. Their bail was set at $3,000 each and neither was able to furnish it.

Five Offenses

Golichnick is charged with extortion on two counts, and check forgery on three. The arrest of this pair followed a series of irregular actions on their part. Golichnick is charged with having written a threat letter to Mrs. G. C. Glaeser demanding $500 and to Joe Balkauskas and to have written several fraudulent checks. Ledden is held as an accessory to the crime, the warrant charging that he had knowledge of Golichnick's activities and that he permitted the use of his automobile, expecting financial returns from Golichnick's work.

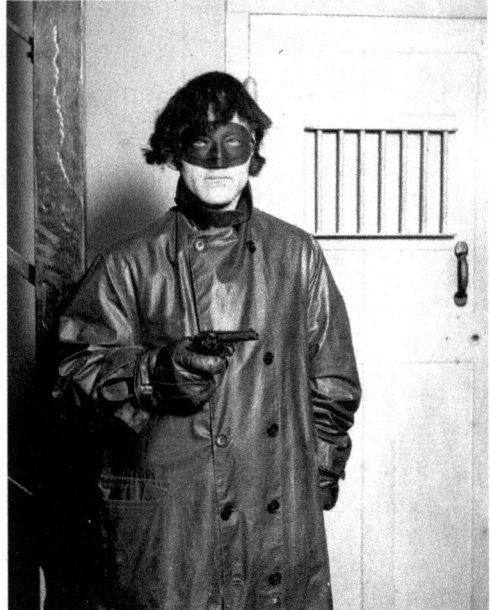

Text of Threat Letter

Following is the text of the threat letter, which Golichnick is alleged to have left at the Glaeser photograph studio, believing he had addressed it to the mother of Miss Dorothy Glaeser, the daughter of Mr. and Mrs. Robert Glaeser.

"Sheboygan, Wis.,"
"March 2, 1929"
"8 A. M."
"Mrs. Glaeser:
Your daughter, Dorothy, is not safely at school as you suppose. My confederates have her in their hands since 11 p.m., yesterday. If you carry out these instructions, no harm will come to her. As soon as you do what is demanded, I

will send my pals a telegram to that effect. You are watched. Go to the bank at 10:00, Draw ($500.00) Dollars in currency. On 8th Street at 12:00 (noon), I expect the money to be put in the mail box of the Coney Island Restaurant opposite the Terminal (street car) depot. This mail box faces the alley outside of the building. Do not inform the police. One suspicious move and your daughter dies. Beware, we are desperate. If money is not there by 12:00, no amount of money afterwards will bring your daughter to life. Scheming will bring remorse. ($500.00 or _____."

"Hickmann II"

The warrant alleged the following:
1. That on March 2, Golichnick "maliciously threatened to do injury to a certain person, namely one Dorothy Glaeser with intent to extort money."
2. That on March 8, he wrote a communication in which he threatened "to do injury to the business of another, namely, the business of Joe Balkauskas with intent thereby to extort money."
3. That on March 9 Golichnick "did utter, publish, pass and tender in payment as true a certain false and forged bank check, knowing the same to be false, and forged with intent to defraud the H.C. Prange company" in the amount of $35, signed Mrs. A. Imig.
4. That on March 9, he tendered a false check signed "Erwin Mohr" in the amount of $50 "with intent to injure and defraud the proprietor of the Traveller's Inn, a soft drink parlor."

5. That on March 9, he tendered another false check for $35 to the H.C. Prange company, signing the name of Mrs. Arthur Imig.

Golichnick and Ledden were arrested Sunday by Detectives Paul Abrahams and Anton Hermann after they had been on the trail for a week. Miss Dorothy Glaeser is a student of the state teacher's college in Milwaukee, and knew nothing of the extortion attempt until informed after the letter was received. She was not disturbed by anyone in Milwaukee, although Golichnick said she was being held.

Golichnick was graduated from the Sheboygan high school with the class of June, 1928. Miss Glaeser was also in that class, and knew Golichnick in school.

Recommends Ordinance Prohibiting Cabarets and All "Cozy Corners"

Sheboygan Press—May 2, 1916

In his annual report to the common council, submitted at the meeting last night, Chief of Police Henry G. Dehne recommended the passage of an ordinance "promoting cabarets and all stue rooms in connection with saloons and cozy corners in candy stores, ice cream parlors and all other public places. Chief Dehne stated that as the city grows larger the immorality increases and he deems it advisable for due council to pass an ordinance to meet these conditions. His report in full follows:

Following is the record of the department for the year April 1, 1915 to April 1, 1916 in detail:

Number of arrests … 674

Number of lodgers given accommodation… 826

Number of male arrests …631

Number of female arrests … 44

Number of patrol calls … 304

Number of sick and injured conveyed…216

Number of miles traveled with patrol and
ambulance … 1560

Number of telephone calls disturbance
suppressed no arrests made …167

Amount of money collected for dog license … 1,712.00

Amount of money collected for officer fees in State and City cases … 1,099.85

Amount of money collected from peddlers & fakirs and merry-go-round …25.00

Amount of money collected for reward and donation for Police Pension fund … 55.00

Amount of money collected for ambulance conveyance … 126.00

Amount of lost and stolen property reported, valued … $3139.26

Amount of lost and stolen property, recovered …1896.58

Number of bicycles stolen … 29

Number of bicycles recovered … 21

Number of lost children returned to parents … 81

Notices served for the city clerk including election notices and posters … 2334

Abusive language ... 37
Absconded from home ...4
Abandonment ...1
Adultery ... 1
Allowing minors to play pool ... 2
Assault and battery ...50
Assault w/intent to do bodily harm ... 1
Bastardy ... 5
Beating board bill ... 4
Burglary ... 7
Cruelty to animals ... 2
Carrying concealed weapons ... 2
Harboring minors in a pool room ... 1
Destroying singing birds ... 2
Demented ... 14
Disorderly conduct ... 133
Drunk ... 65
Drunk and disorderly ... 89
Embezzlement ... 2
Forgery ... 7
Gambling ... 19

Fornication ... 3
Interfering with an officer ... 3
Issuing worthless checks ... 3
Incorrigible ... 1
Keeping house of ill-fame ... 1
Larceny Petit ... 55
Larceny Grand ... 1
Mayhem ... 1
Man Slaughter ... 1
Nonsupport ...8
Peace warrant ... 4
Peddling without license ... 3
Procuring liquor to minors ... 2
Prostitute ... 1
Selling liquor to minors ... 2
Selling cigarettes to minors ... 3
Suspicion ... 39
Reckless driving ... 2
Receiving stolen property ... 2

First City of Sheboygan Police Department

Ice Cream Parlor Evils

Sheboygan Press Telegram—October 3, 1925

Some question has been raised with reference to adopting Alderman Sonnemann's proposed ordinance to have all places where non-intoxicating beverages are sold under license or permit, closed at 12 o'clock midnight, and remain closed until daylight the following day.

But in the light of recent exposures this ordinance should be approved by the entire Common Council, and every such licensed person who is living within the law can endorse it, for there is little or no legal business done after midnight. The proposed ordinance aims to hit the law violators, and it is worthy of the unanimous action of the Common Council.

If it serves no other purpose, it will close a number of so-called ice cream parlors which have become a menace to Sheboygan and which are doing more to corrupt the morals than any other one influence that is at work in the city at this time.

Evidence is at hand of certain ice cream parlors that are dispensing liquor and in some instances young girls have reeled out of these places under the influence of what has been sold there. These so-called places that are complained of, have become rendezvous for liquor parties and girls of a tender age are frequently in these places at late hours with male companions when they ought to be home under the influence of their parents. Not only is liquor being sold in these Class B places in direct violation of the law, but booths are maintained in direct conflict with the city ordinance, and "petting parties" are frequent.

Some months ago a man about sixty years of age had two girls in one of these booths, neither one over fifteen year of age, and was giving them booze from a silver flask.. It is conditions like these that are corrupting the morals of Sheboygan, and these are the places that want to keep open into the early hours of morning. No ice cream parlor or confectionery store, dealing in sweets and living within the full meaning of the law, will keep its doors open longer than midnight, and law-abiding ones are closing up at 11 o'clock.

This ordinance should be adopted if for no other reason than to remedy certain class B places in the city of Sheboygan. It may be argued that if we close the places, we will drive the young people out into the rural sections, but this can be easily be remedied by working in harmony with the County Board which convenes within the next two weeks, and action should be taken whereby a county wide ban will be in force.

Under the present situation a girl can stay out until 1 or 2 o'clock in the morning and then offer the alibi that she was in one of these ice cream parlors, and this explanation in the main satisfies, but if these places were closed at midnight it would be a different story.

When the County Board convenes it will have an important duty to perform, that of adopting a resolution that will regulate dances throughout the county, and the Common Council and the board should plan to work out some kind of an ordinance which will protect both the city and the country, one adopted by the Council, and a similar one by the County Board, it will go a long way towards improving the situation.

But in the meantime there is no necessity to delay rigid action so far as these Class B places are concerned where knowledge is at hand of liquor being sold. The Mayor and Common Council should revoke every one of these Class B permits or insist that the law be lived up to and places closed at a reasonable hour. People seeking amusement are not out looking for ice cream and soft drinks at 1 and 2 o'clock in the morning.

We have a dozen or more ice cream parlors that are living within the law, closing early and it is an outrage that a certain few, utterly ignoring the law, should be the means of creating a condition which calls for rigid action. A newspaper is not for entertainment. It has a given mission to perform as the writer views it, and unless it exercises that right and privilege it fails in its duty.

Jahn Found Innocent of Embezzling Ducks

The Sheboygan Press — July 20, 1955

Juneau (AP) - Dr Laurence Jahn, chief waterfowl biologist of the Wisconsin Conservation Department, was found innocent of embezzling ducks discarded from his experimental breeding pens Tuesday night by a Circuit Court jury that deliberated less than 90 minutes.

The acquittal wound up nearly two years of controversy during which three young game management experts of the department were accused by department wardens of unlawfully conducting research work on pen-reared birds.

Richard Hunt, another Horicon biologist, was charged with illegal possession of migratory waterfowl last year, with Warden Ken Beghin — who testified he ate an illegal duck as guest of one biologist — the complainant. The case was dismissed upon testimony that the birds were pen-reared ducks, not wild birds.

Similar charges then were dismissed against Keith White, and a warrant once issued for Dr. Jahn by former Dodge County Dist. Atty. John Kaiser was withdrawn.

Appeal Pending

However, this year Kaiser's successor, Dist. Atty. Bruce Rasmussen, brought the more serious embezzlement charge against Jahn, a nationally recognized authority on waterfowl.

Specifically, Jahn was charged with giving six culled birds from the pen to his father, Roy, of Lake Mills. The elder Jahn was hustled to a Jefferson County justice court in 1954 and fined but appealed and the case is still pending.

Neither Jahn nor the other biologists denied culling the unwanted birds from their research pens, pointing out that disposing of specimens unwanted in further breeding tests was part of their project.

Jahn's superior in the game management division, wildlife research chief Cyril Kabat, testified in Tuesday's brief defense presentation that Jahn had the authority to dispose of unwanted birds in any way he saw fit.

Prosecution testimony showed that Jahn had crated number of culled birds but that all died-except the six he gave his father.

Completion of the legal maneuvering involving the three young management experts cleared the way for the thorough investigation Conservation Director L. P. Voigt has promised into the situation.

Disloyal Utterance Brings Eviction
And Fine To Kohler Man

Sheboygan Press — February 20, 1918

"The Austrians can lick the Americans to a frazzle," said Robert Lachinsky of Kohler.

"Ten dollars and costs," said Justice of the Peace Adam Trester.

Lachinsky was arrested by the constable of Kohler on the complaint of Fred Retzlaff, proprietor of a saloon and boarding house at that village. The statement of Lachinsky precipitated a young riot in which Retzlaff had the misfortune to have his shirt torn to shreds and the undesirable on was ejected from the saloon. He was said to be somewhat under the influence of liquor and when explaining the matter to Justice Trester late yesterday afternoon said that he merely made the remark to tease the bartender.

The defendant was given a lecture by the justice and warned not to repeat the offense. He separated himself from the fine and costs amounting to $19.62.

Steals A Pair Of Shoes

Sheboygan Press — July 8, 1911

Matt Urban, a Lithuanian, stole a pair of shoes Friday. He might have stolen several hundred dollars worth of checks but he had no need of them. He did however need the shoes; all good citizens and well dressed men do. The shoes however cost him a great deal more than their intrinsic value. He was fined five dollars and costs for the offense in all amounting to ten dollars and eight cents. His financial condition was not of the best, however, so he took twenty days in the county jail and gave up the shoes also.

Now, this aforesaid Mr. Urban had been looking for work Friday. He went to the office of the Parlor Frame Company to get a job. No one was in the office — a pair of shoes and a large number of checks were there. Passing up the latter he took the shoes and disappeared. Complaint was made and Matt was found with the shoes. He wanted both the shoes and work — but the fates are not so bountiful. Now he has the work (on the stone pile) but it minus the shoes.

SOME BIG
AND LITTLE
TRAMPS

Charles Skuip, a Wandering Willie, with an army of followers stronger than Coxey ever had, marched into the police station Sunday. He was attired in about three suits of clothes, or at least they were suits once upon a time. Besides holding his own body they covered the bodies of at least a thousand young vags of the four legged type. Judge Giblin in passing sentence, only had jurisdiction over the larger tramp but the little fellows accompanied him and with a bath took a scramble for the sewer mains.

Sheboygan Press—
December 14, 1911

First Fire Station and Jail in Oostburg

Sheboygan Press —
June 3, 1912

HORSE AND BUGGY STOLEN FROM BARN

John Rooney, a well known resident of Town Mitchell, had a valuable horse and buggy stolen from his barn last night. Warrants have been issued and the guilty party or parties are expected to be apprehended in a short time.

****This is not the stolen buggy, horse or the thief

Sheboygan Press — September 15, 1913

Two Burglars and a Horse Thief Enter Plea of Guilty in Circuit Court this Afternoon--Famous Ott Case Here for Trial.

Hardened as criminals, showing evidence of crime in their bearing before the court. Ignatz Nagli, Henry Fellberg and Charles Maier, appeared before Judge Kirwan and entered pleas of guilty to the charges in the complaints. Edwin Dobbratz, charged with stealing money from his uncle in Sheboygan Falls, and who was arrested at Stillwater, Minn., by Sheriff Fischer entered a plea of guilty but the court refused to accept this until his father appeared and at 10 o'clock tomorrow morning he will be arraigned for the second charge. Nagli is up for horse stealing, Fellberg and Maier for burglary, the latter stealing a watch from Mrs. Eimerman, residing near Elkhart Lake. Fellberg and Nagli besides the crimes referred to are jail breakers, and were captured some weeks ago by the Deputy Sheriff at Random Lake.

The remainder of the criminal calendar will be taken up at 2 o'clock tomorrow afternoon and those entering pleas of guilty will be sentenced at the close of the term.

In 1730, £20 was offered in New York for the capture of a horse thief.

17

"Rub-A-Dub-Dub Three Fools in a tub. And who do you think they be?" Well, not quite...

Three Men in Boat in Jail Now

February 16, 1924

Three Trenton (N.J.) men claimed they were out fishing and caught several sacks of booze. Cops said the booze part sounded fishy and the fishing part sounded boozy.

Fisherman, as you may know, await their catch with bated breath Well, these three men's breath was bombed. The serious-minded judge intimated they were rum runners, and that the only fish they wanted were suckers.

Such is the tale of three men in a boat. They caught not suckers, but hades.

Wife and Her Ex-Husband Jail Inmates

Sheboygan Press — March 10, 1925

Fred Schillingowski and his divorced wife, Mrs. Lydia Schillingowski, have set a precedent at the county jail.

This is the first time that a husband and wife, or to be exact, a divorced husband and wife, have been inmates of the county jail at the same time. Fred Schillingowski has been confined there since January 1, while awaiting trial in circuit court on the charges of failure to pay alimony. His former wife was sentenced to a 106-day jail term by Judge Meyer Monday afternoon for being guilty of conducting a disorderly house.

In the meantime the six children are without a father or mother. The oldest of these is 12 years, and the youngest is only three and a half month.

NO TIRE TROUBLE IN THE DRUNKEN DRIVERS HOME

-THE LITTLE HOUSE ON THE HILL-
FOR THE BENEFIT OF THOSE WHO
MAY NOT RECOGNIZE THE BUILDING IN THIS
SKETCH WE WILL EXPLAIN-IT IS THE
PLACE WHERE THE $50 AND 60 DAYS
BOYS RESIDE

Oostburg Man Mistaken For John Dillinger

Sheboygan Press—March 13, 1934

Oostburg (Special) — Jack Fass, head of the Indian Mound Products company here, would be personally relieved if the police would recapture John Dillinger, the notorious killer and bank robber, who escaped recently from the jail at Crown Point.

Mr. Fass, who happens to bear resemblance to Dillinger, has been inconvenienced half a dozen times by being mistaken for Dillinger since the outlaw has been at large. He hopes the case of mistaken identity doesn't ever get beyond the point of inconvenience. Thus far he has been able to convince his "captors" that he is not the man they are seeking.

Only this week, on a business trip to Milwaukee, Mr. Fass was stopped twice, once by a policeman in the downtown section of the city and once by squad car which pursued his automobile to the city limits. The second time, after five policemen had covered him with revolvers and ordered him to get out of his car. Mr. Fass confessed that the business of establishing his identity has passed the amusement stage and is getting to be something of an ordeal.

Brutally Murdered

For a Fortune Which Did Not Exist

John Sexton's name hit the front page headlines of Sheboygan County newspapers June 29, 1911. Sexton, a pioneer schoolteacher of Elkhart Lake, was brutally murdered in 1911 for a fortune he never accumulated.

Sexton lived just outside what is today the entrance to the Sheboygan Marsh. A historic marker stands on the site of his home. Sexton arrived in the area in 1845 from his native Vermont. He became the town's first teacher, clerk and postmaster. Living alone, and something of a recluse since the death of his wife, the old man was well respected in the neighborhood, a friend to all.

On the evening of June 28th, Joseph Flath, a neighbor of John's, found Sexton stabbed and beaten in his cottage. After a search of the area a bloody knife was found nearby. No other clues were in evidence until two days later when the employer of a group of Italian laborers at the Sheboygan Marsh reported three of his men missing, among them a man named Anthony Borillo. After a search of Borillo's rooms, John Sexton's watch was discovered.

In that summer of 1911 a group of Italian workers was hired to work at the Marsh and a nearby quarry on improvement projects, and it seems a small group of these young men believed in the myth that John Sexton's home hid, among its hoards, a fortune.

Led by Tony Borillo, the group committed the heinous crime and fled first to Chicago, then back to Naples, Italy. The men had managed to steal about three hundred dollars, not in cash, but in certificates of deposit and when they were used to purchase steamer tickets to Italy, the game was up.

The Sheboygan County Board of Supervisors pledged a $1000 reward and Governor Francis McGovern, once a local teacher, offered $300 of is own for the capture of the perpetrators.

Cooperating with local police Italian officials caught Borillo in September of 1911 on a farm two hundred miles outside of Naples. They captured him after a

vicious battle. Two local officers traveled to Rome to bring him back, but extradition was denied by the Italian government, so they came home empty-handed.

Rome agreed to try Borillo and sentenced him to seventeen years in prison. He died in prison while serving time for Sexton's murder.

Frighteningly, Borillo was reputed to have been one of the leaders of the Camorra gang, which terrorized Italy in the early 1900s.

A historical marker was erected in 1941 at the site of John Sexton's home. The old homestead stood until 1938 when it was razed.

Sexton is buried in Walnut Grove Cemetery on a hill overlooking Glenbeulah. The Rev. Mr. Schuetze, who preached the sermon at Sexton's funeral, referred to him as a "man of education, of science, the helpful and good neighbor and a man of confiding and loving heart."

, WIS., SATURDAY EVENING, JULY 8, 1911 .

ASSIST IN CAPTURING THE MURDERER

The Press believes that the reward should be increased to $1000 or more for the apprehension of the murderer or murderers of John L. Sexton, and to that end a blank form is being run in this paper. Fill out this blank with the amount you wish to contribute and mail to this office. The amount subscribed will be listed in this paper and each will be a certificate calling for the amount set opposite your name to be paid only in case of the arrest and conviction of the murderer or murderers of this old man. You can aid in the work by increasing the reward. The larger the reward the greater activity on the part of the officers of the country to apprehend the guilty person or persons. Don't delay but fill out the blank today and mail it to this office.

Sheboygan, Wis.

$...............

I hereby pledge the amount set opposite my name towards a Reward Fund for the apprehending of the murderer of John L. Sexton and will honor this certificate when it is presented to me for the sum pledged.

It is understood that I am in no way obligated unless there is an arrest and conviction of the murderer.

Signed........................... ... .

Dated 1911

21

JOHN L. SEXTON
FOULLY MURDERED

Mr. J. L. Sexton Meets Death by an Assassin's Hands—The Murder Clouded in Mystery—Thought to Have Been Committed for Money It was Supposed He Possessed

Headlines on June 29, 2011 in Sheboygan

Workmen Setting Up Sexton Marker At Marsh

SITE OF
FORMER HOME
OF
JOHN L. SEXTON
PIONEER SCHOOL TEACHER
A friend of the
Great Outdoors
Born 1824. Died 1911

Workmen are seen here erecting the Sexton marker at the Sheboygan marsh. Left to right, Charles Sorenson, Otto Ackerman, Sebastian Platzer, Emil Reinbacher, who made the marker, and Joe Meyer, foreman on the job. The marker is placed 150 feet north of the Sexton property line, adjacent to where the old homestead stood until torn down three years ago. The spot is landscaped with fine trees and makes an ideal setting for the marker.

1941

READS LIKE FICTION
BUT IS STRANGER

The Hermit, J. L. Sexton, Who Was So Cruelly Murdered in 1911 in His Humble Home in the Town of Russell, Makes a Confession, So It Is Reported in a Periodical Published in St. Louis — Told Rev. Fischer, Who Was Pastor of the Russell Church, How He Killed Two in England and Fled the Country—Came from a Family of Noblemen.

Sexton Trivia

An avid reader and nature lover, John Sexton was a Thoreau or Emerson of his day, an educated scholar who wrote homespun philosophies and opinions. Some of his favorite topics included God and man, fire, the intelligence of animals and his neighbors like Indian John.

He wrote of the discovery of submerging burning skin in cold water to avoid blisters when he received a bad burn to his hand. He also observed the intelligence of his hog.

An interesting friendship existed between Sexton and millionaire Matthias Gottfried of Elkhart Lake. What a picture it would have made to see the well-groomed Gottfried, owner of a mansion , standing alongside the unkempt, bushy, long-bearded and long-haired Sexton (who at one time claimed to have skipped a haircut for twenty-five years) with eyebrows that stood out proud and fierce, humble dweller of a crude, one –room cottage.

Among piles of papers, books and magazines, Sexton wrote his opinions about money and happiness. "Many are grasping to accumulate wealth, thinking that to be the chief cornerstone of human felicity. But are they not mistaken? Have we any evidence that they who make wealth are in the end most happy?

Sexton lived in peaceful poverty, but rumors of Sexton being a wealthy man tempted an Italian immigrant working in a lime quarry in the nearby Sheboygan Marsh area.

John Sexton's tombstone reads, Gone, But Not Forgotten. His grave has a clear view of the Sheboygan Marsh he so dearly loved.

THE AUBURN MYSTERY

Fond du Lac Commonwealth Reporter   May 10, 1884

The correspondent in Auburn has furnished the Commonwealth with the following account of the evidence in the Fox case, concerning which there is so much interest and so little known. He says that if Mr. McCroary had attended an examination at Dundee, Mr. Fox would undoubtedly have been bound over for trial, as he secured an attorney, and the state had none. The account is evidently written by one who seems to be the only version of the affair obtainable. The account is as follows:

First, many believe that Fox was smart enough to put his wife where she could not be touched with an ordinary boat paddle or stick, and that is about all that the searchers had when looking for the lost, the hook and rope being useless on account of the pond lily roots. Some went there to see what they could see, smoke their pipes, and probably talk something else.

The circumstantial evidence that has been found is as follows: A son of John Slattery called at Fox's for something, the boy being a great friend of Mrs. Fox. Not seeing Mrs. Fox, he asked Fox where she was. Mr. Fox said she had gone to a neighbor's to get her hair combed. The son of Mr. Slattery then asked how long she had been gone and Fox said, nine days. It probably would have been ninety days if the boy had not come and asked for her. In a day or so he gets the same Slattery boy to search for her, and goes up to the county line looking for her, but no Mrs. Fox has been there.

Mrs. Fox was seen at her home by Joseph Kayser of the Town of Scott in the latter part of March. She was hardly able to walk in the house, to say nothing of walking over half a mile to her nearest neighbors. She showed Mr. Kayser her feet and they were swelled up so that she could not put on her shoes. Between the 2t6th and 28th of March Mr. Stokes was building a fence on a piece of land adjoining Fox's and when he was at work he heard the two, Fox and his wife having a terrible quarrel, and all at once everything was quiet and there was nothing heard after that. That same afternoon, Fox went to a neighbor of his, Mr. Kelling, with an abstract of his, or some of his land to sell it to him. Mrs. Kelling noticed that Fox was very uneasy about something and did not make a very long stay. Don't forget this land he wanted to sell he got deeded over to someone in your city, for the purpose probably that after Mrs. Fox was out of the way, there would be no trouble getting all the cash and skip, and that is what he will do if the slack officials dally any longer.

Mrs. Fox had four or five pet dogs, and when she went anywhere, there would generally at least three go with her. All the dogs are now at home. And had she laid down voluntarily, or otherwise, the dogs would have caused immediate alarm.

A day or so after the Slattery boy had been at the house of Fox, he, Fox called at the home of Mr. Slattery, and stayed till quite late in the evening. Mr. Slattery invited him to stay with them, it being lonesome without his wife. "No," said Fox, "I must go home." The next day or so he came again to Mr. Slattery's and made the remark that he wished he had stayed with them that night, for he saw a devil in every corner of his house. Why did he see those devils? Surely not because his wife had gone to get her hair combed.

There is plenty of evidence that will, in time, undoubtedly come out, for it is believed by nine persons out of every ten in the neighborhood that Mrs. Fox never left the premises alive, and some even believe that he cremated her. It is a known fact that the house they lived in was so filthy that the threshers would hardly eat at their house. But, since the search has been made for Mrs. Fox, the parties that were with the crowd noticed the floor had been mopped and scoured. It he did cremate her, and some scientific men would take a hold, they would undoubtedly find what remains. But, the fact of the matter is Fox had ample time to make sure to hide any residue.

Town of Auburn, Fond du Lac County 1862

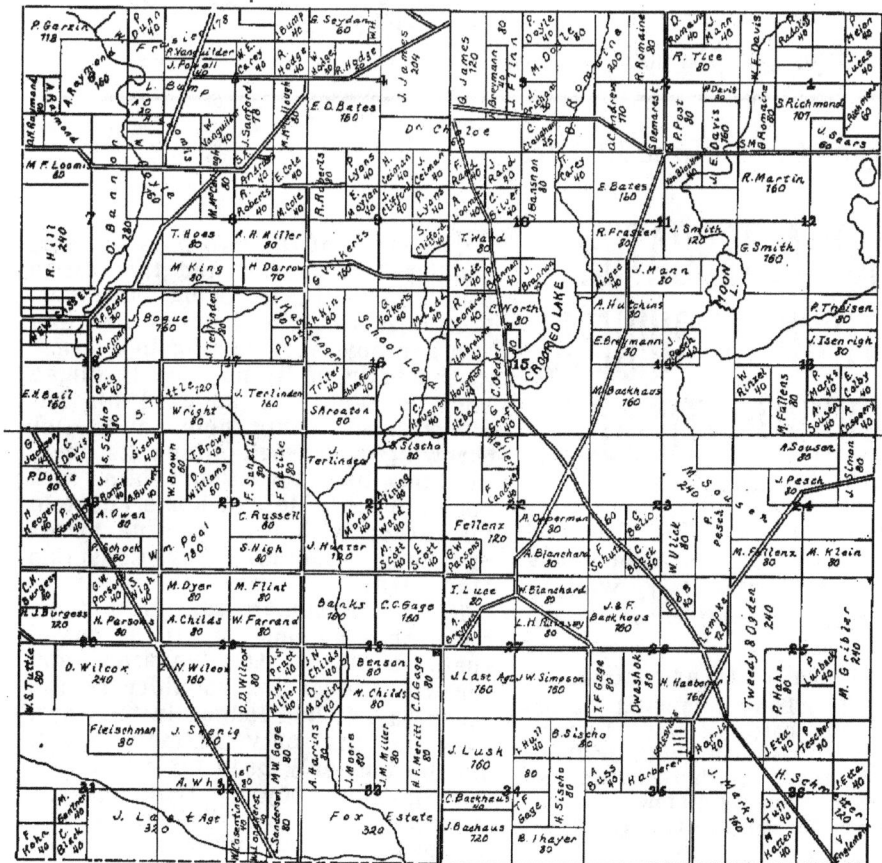

25

Manitowoc Herald Times— January 7, 1961

Smart Guy Lands in Jail

SHEBOYGAN (AP)—A 25-year old man who sent police a postcard saying they weren't smart enough to catch him appeared in Circuit Court Friday and pleaded guilty to 14 charges.

He's Ray Ohm Jr., of Sheboygan, who was returned to the County Jail pending a pre-sentence investigation ordered by Judge F. H. Schlicting. Ohm was returned to a cell when unable to post bond of $12,000.

The charges included one of non-support, nine of check forgery, three of larceny and one of aggravated assault. The assault charge stemmed from an attack on his wife because she refused to kiss him during a jail visit earlier in the week.

Ohm, a parolee from the State Reformatory, left town Nov. 30 after cashing $367 worth of bad checks. He sent a card from California saying there wasn't "anyone on the police force intelligent enough to catch me." He returned to Wisconsin a short while later and was arrested in a nearby tavern.

Sheboygan Prsss— June 12, 1923

BOYISH ALTERCATION IN TOWN OF RHINE IS BROUGHT INTO COURT

A neighborhood difference between boys in the town of Rhine was aired in Justice Harry Wolters' court yesterday afternoon when Roland Bushman, 18 years, was fined $5 and costs amounting to about $15. The complaint of assault and battery was brought against the Bushman youth by Robt. Hartman, town of Rhine farmer, as a result of what he claimed was an attack on his boy, Leroy Hartman, 11 years.

The story of the two boys in court conflicted somewhat and the justice was lenient in imposing the fine. Leroy Hartman told of he who and another boy were fishing in a creek in the town of Rhine. The Bushman boy, he said, had knocked his hat off with a fishing pole and after throwing a mussel, minus its shell, at him, had threatened him with bodily injury. He ran home and told his father with the resulting arrest of young Bushman by Constable Marquardt.

Roland Bushman said in his defense that he had opened a mussel shell, taken out the "innards" and thrown it over his shoulder at the other boy. It had lodged in the boy's overalls, the only garment, worn, and he had only been trying to help the Hartman boy by removing his overalls for him. His story was borne out by the other boy.

Sheboygan Press — July 15, 1908

BOYS IMITATE GOATS

Three Boys Arrested for Crying B-a-a-h at a Neighbor

HOFFMANN IS THE VICTIM

Richard Hoffmann Doesn't Want to be Taken for a Goat. Goat Crys Grate on His Nerves

Just because several boys persisted in imitating goats and yelling B-a-a-h, B-a-a-h, everytime that any member of Richard Hoffmann's family was within hearing distance, a law suit is now being fought.

Some short time ago the Hoffmann's bought several goats which created a great deal of amusement to the children of the neighborhood. The boys and girls would come frequently to tease the strange animals. Finally this became such a nuisance that the Hoffmanns ordered them to stop.

The children enraged that one of their favorite pleasures had been denied them planned revenge. So every time that they saw a member of the Hoffmann family they uttered the crys of a goat.

The older members of the community considered the joke a good one and followed in the steps of the children, so the north side sounded as if it were the feeding grounds of a herd of goats.

The Hoffmans complained and three boys ranging from seventeen to twenty were arrested.

Sheboygan Press — April 19, 1915

FATHER AT 78 GIVES SON OF 50 A BEATING

JOHN SCHWARTZ ARRESTED SATURDAY NIGHT BY THE SHERIFF

Although 78 years old and his hair white as snow, John Schwartz, a farmer residing in the southern part of the city, Saturday night inflicted a severe beating on his son, Hans Schwartz, aged 50 years.

Family troubles are said to have been responsible for the quarrel at the home of the son on South Ninth street, followed by a fist fight. The father knocked the son to the floor, and then, according to his own statement, kicked his son in the head.

A telephone call to the sheriff's office announcing that "somebody was being murdered" caused Sheriff Kreuter and Deputy Sheriff George Goodell to make a flying trip to the scene in an automobile. They placed the aged man under arrest.

The son was covered with blood when they reached his home, but after receiving medical attention he was found to be in no serious condition. A charge of assault and battery was instituted on complaint of the son.

Before Justice Treater this morning the senior Schwartz was fined $5 and costs which was paid by the son whom he had chastised, and the two left the court room together.

Sheboygan Press—November 13, 1915

DEPREDATIONS CAUSE ACTION BY THE POLICE

The police are investigating reported depredations in the northeast section of the city. For the past week a number of complaints have been received at police headquarters to the effect that outhouses were being turned over, windows broken and other outrages committed.

The latest report is from the home of J. Verhage, Lincoln avenue, whose windows were broken in with cabbage heads. The cabbage was stolen from a nearby garden. Chickens were stolen from the coop of Phillip Fields on Lighthouse Court and a horse was released from the barn of Martin DeVriend, and was found wandering on the streets later.

Prosecutions will follow the possible arrest of the guilty parties.

Cruelty to Animals and Violation of Section 1,561 R. S.

Last Sunday Wm. Guhl, of the city hired a "rig" of a city liveryman and invited his friend Mike Esser to take a ride. Each took in for ballast a cargo of bock beer and started for this moral and intellectual suburb of the city of chairs and children. The ordinary pace of a faithful and well bred horse was not satisfactory to the disciples of Gambrinus who were riding after it, and the driver lashed it into a run; coming into town at a furious gait, and driving through the streets in a manner dangerous to pedestrians, and shocking to the refined sensibilities of the inhabitants. The cruel bipeds were arrested, and Monday morning Esquire Pierce took out his scales and placed law and justice on one side, and the prisoners on the other, and on a plea of "guilty," the pair were assessed a fine of $4.00 each with costs amounting to $5.18 for Esser, and $8.61 for Guhl, and in addition, Guhl was required to partake of the hospitalities of Mine Host, Mueller, for five days at his brick tavern where the windows are furnished with iron musquito netting: and in case the fine and costs be not paid, to abide for a time longer, not to exceed ten days additional. Esser stepped to the front with cash and Guhl when last seen here was seated with Marshal Garton behind a spirited gray stepper belonging to the Marshal, and apparently the officer was taking his friend down to get a view of Lake Michigan and locate him near the shore where the swish swash of the wild waves may calm the perturbed spirit of the violater of the statutes "in such case made and provided." Next!! 5-23-1888

Sheboygan Press — November 18, 1936

By Way Of Report

Excitement ran high on Sheboygan's northeast side the other night when a prominent citizen thought he spotted a "brown bear" in the streets. A call to the police department brought a squad car to the scene, and a policeman was all set to shoot when another officer discovered that the "bear" was just a huge dog

[And that's not just the bear story either]

The Story of Louie Eisold's Demise

Sheboygan Herald—
October 10, 1886
Louis Eisold who was
struck with a beer glass by
Wm. Schaetzer during a
quarrel in the saloon of Hermann & Kroos in the 4th
ward a week ago Sunday
(September 26), died last
Sunday afternoon (October
3). Schaetzer was arrested
about 9 o'clock Sunday
evening and placed under
$500 bonds to await trial.

Eisold Family

Eisold worked a part of last week and there appears to be a question as to whether his death was caused by the blow from the glass. It is also claimed that Eisold
attacked Schaetzer first with a chair.

Sheboygan Herald—October 16, 1886
A week ago last Sunday at Kroos & Heermann's saloon in the 4th ward Louis
Eishold and Wm. Schaetzer quarreled about some trifling matter and during a
struggle that ensued Schaetzer struck Eishold over the head with a beer mug.
Eishold was taken to Dr. Bock's drug store, the would dressed and the next day
went to work; but Tuesday he complained of pain in his head and quit work
about noon; his head grew worse and he died the Sunday following at 3 o'clock
p.m. Schaetzer was then arrested and placed under $500 bonds, and is now out
on bail. Drs. Bock and Gunther held a post-mortem examination and a coroner's
jury brought in a verdict to the effect that he came to his death from the effect of
the blow upon his head. Deceased was born in 1847 in Germany and leaves a
wife and four children. Schaetzer is also married and has a family.

Sheboygan Herald—October 30, 1886
Wm. Schaetzer chared with being the cause of Louis Eishold's death from striking him with a beer glass has been bound over to the Circuit Court under bonds
of $5,000; he secured bondsmen and is now out on bail.

Jim McCabe and Mike Bieser of the Milwaukee Ale House, "after sifting
through the hand written records that were fire damaged from a courthouse fire"
they found that "Louie had it coming" and the fight was over a woman. He was

29

picking a fight with another bar patron over the man's wife. After the scuffle moved outside, Louie was sent on his way bruised up. Near closing time Louie came back. A fight escalated and Schaetzer clocked Louie with the beer glass.

Legend has it, an onlooker pried the beer from Louie's dying hands and toasted his lustful life.

Love Leads to Murder

During the evening of July 25, 1928, two ex-husbands of thrice-married Anna Masiulonis, Joseph Masiulonis and William Rutches, engaged in a bloody knife fight which resulted in the death of Rutches from loss of blood from multiple stab wounds.

Masiulonis was visiting his ex-wife, who was divorcing him, when Rutches showed up and the two began to fight. The beginnings of the fight were witnessed by Anna Masiulonis and her daughter, Margaret Zamizamski, 13, who fled to a neighbor's house. Neighbors ignored her cries for help and refused to call the police.

When Mrs. Maiulonis and daughter returned to their home, everything was quiet so they went to bed. They were awaken the next morning by the shouts of neighbors who had found Ruthches body.

Masiulonis was charged with second degree murder and was put on trial in September. He was found guilty and sentenced to 14-16 years at Waupun. It

---

Officer Killed

The first policeman killed in the line of duty in Sheboygan was special police officer Charles Freiher who was struck by a switch engine, thrown under the cars and killed instantly on September 7, 1895.

Freiher was working the last night of a two-month special duty assignment substituting for police officers who were on vacation.

He caught sight of a man stepping out of the blind baggage car, and thinking him a non-paying customer, started across the tracks to arrest him. Several witnesses shouted a warning, but Freiher never saw the engine.

Gambling and Vice

Over the years, Sheboygan County, has had its share of businesses that engaged in illegal gambling and prostitution. Many of these businesses were taverns that engaged in legitimate moneymaking activities, but sought alternative ways to increase their legal trade as well as earning a little extra "on the side". Periodically, the Law would conduct raids, in which they would confiscate gambling equipment, or occasionally an individual would be arrested for keeping a house of ill fame. After a short time everything would be back to business as usual. It was not until the 1950s, that there was any real crack-down on gambling or prostitution. With the election of a new, aggressive district attorney, the process of cleaning up the county had begun.

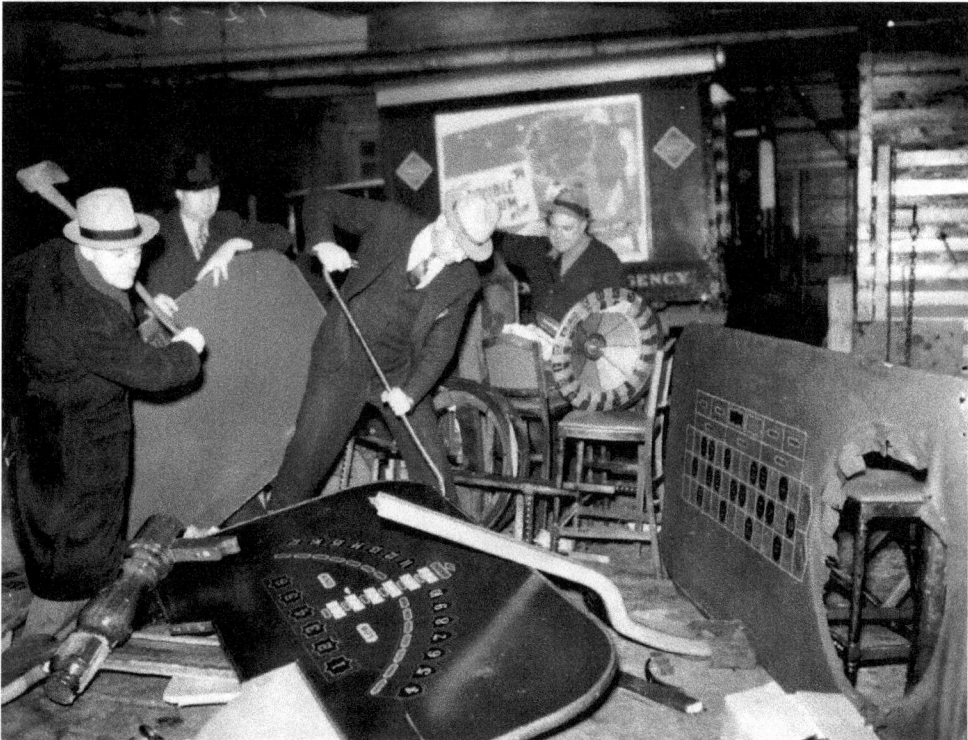

Sheriff Joe Dreps and aides destroy confiscated gambling equipment taken from the Paddock Club in Elkhart Lake in the early 1930s.

Slot machines and gambling equipment are burned after raids on gambling establishments in the 1930s. (September 7, 1938 below)

Gambling Equipment Seized In Raid At Elkhart

Above photo shows the gambling and bar equipment confiscated by the sheriff's department after the raid on the Paddock club at Elkhart Lake early Sunday morning. In the foreground is the roulette wheel, to the left is a large roulette table and directly behind the roulette wheel is a crap game board, with another roulette table behind it. The equipment and gaming devices are stored under guard in the Hensel Transfer and Warehousing company building, 530 N. Seventh street.

Paddock Club At Elkhart Is Raided By Sheriff's Men

Complainant And Others At Elkhart Lake Request The Protection Of Deputies From Tom Hanley

Three residents of Elkhart Lake today demanded protection by sheriff's deputies from Tom Hanley, proprietor of the Paddock club at Elkhart Lake which was raided for gambling by sheriff's deputies early Monday morning.

The demands were made of Sheriff Joseph Dreps immediately after Hanley appeared in Justice Clarence La Du's court at Sheboygan Falls and it was found that the case would have to be adjourned to 10 a. m. Wednesday owing to District Attorney Jacob A. Fessler's absence from the city. Those who asked protection were William Zeller, bartender at Siebken's resort and one of the signers of the complaint against the Paddock club, August Stark of Pine Point resort, and Henry Wurtz, a food broker at Elkhart Lake.

Sheriff Dreps said that the men will be given protection by deputies after hearing charges by Mr. Zeller that Hanley had entered the Siebken resort bar and roughed him because of anger over the raid.

Secured Warrant

Sheriff Dreps and his deputies first attempted to raid the Paddock club Saturday night after complaints had been made over long distance telephone by a number of resorters. He immediately went to the club, but was refused admission without a search warrant and was told "This is a private party." Owing to the absence of the district attorney, the sheriff was handicapped legally, but he finally recured a warrant from Justice George Goodell and staged the raid early Monday morning when he seized some dice boxes and a roulette table covering as evidence. Pending the district attorney's return, Sheriff Dreps said he would have to secure legal advice on what action to pursue, and as a result the case was adjourned to tomorrow.

It was at this point that the Elkhart men asked for protection. Mr. Zeller displayed a bandaged left hand and told the sheriff that following the raid Hanley had come into the Siebken place and started a fight with him. After Justice LaDu adjourned the case, Mr. Zeller and Mr. Hanley had to be held apart in order to avoid coming to blows.

Joe Ryan Fined $100 By Justice

State Wins Victory In Court — Defense Is Filing An Appeal To Circuit Court

Joe Ryan of Milwaukee, proprietor of the Paddock club at Elkhart Lake, was found guilty of possession of alleged gambling apparatus and fined $100 and costs or six months in county jail by Justice Aaron Mael in Sheboygan Falls this morning.

Counsel for the defense, Attorney A. H. Gruhle, Sheboygan, and Cornelius Hanley, Milwaukee, immediately filed an appeal to the circuit court, because their motion for quashing of evidence and suppression of the search warrant was denied by the court.

District Attorney Jacob A. Fessler, counsel for the state, made a dramatic appeal to the court against "this vicious vice of gambling that is practically ruining the business in the county.

The defendant's bond remained at $150, as set by the court Jui, 6.

Plea To Court

"I say to this court," Mr. Fessler declared, "that it is its duty to aid the district attorney, the sheriff and all law abiding citizens in the complete stamping out and suppression of all forms of gambling in the county of Sheboygan. We must, repeat, it is imperative, get rid of vice and gambling. The morals of Sheboygan are at stake We as officers of the county of Sheboygan would be derelict in our sworn duty if we did not go the full length of the law in rooting out this cancerous growth of gambling that is eating at the very foundations of good, clean, wholesome business and recreation in Sheboygan county."

The district attorney, pounding out his words on the table, declared that "the court cannot show any leniency in the disposition of this case. This case must be a lesson to all people in this city, in this county, or in this state that we of Sheboygan county will not stand for any further violation of our laws. I intend to see to it personally that all clues in our possession relating to gambling or any other form of vice will be hunted to the root and that root destroyed, completely and absolutely."

Grand Jury Investigation Is Requested By Petition

A petition asking a grand jury investigation of alleged gambling and vice conditions in Sheboygan county is being circulated here at the present time by members of a citizenship committee, The petition reads as follows

"It is a matter of general belief that commercialized vice and gambling are flagrantly prevalent in this community. We are informed that private investigations have largely substantiated this belief and that citizens have appealed to the law enforcement officials of the county without success.

"It is important to the self-respect of our community and its good name elsewhere that the facts be determined officially and any violations of the law be punished.

"We, the undersigned residents of Sheboygan county, do therefore respectfully petition the judge of the circuit court to impanel a grand jury which can proceed promptly and thoroughly to investigate the alleged conditions."

Rev. Oscar Adam, pastor of the First Methodist Episcopal church in Sheboygan, who authorized the statement Monday night that 21 ministers of the county had announced their endorsement of the citizenship committee's activities, stated today that no chairman of the citizenship committee had been publicly named as yet. He said he acted as chairman at the meeting of ministers, but is not chairman of the citizenship committee.

July 1938

THREE INJURED BY EXPLOSION

ATTEMPT TO DRY OUT DYNAMITE PROVES FATAL

William Klein was probably fatally injured and two others seriously hurt in a dynamite explosion which occurred Monday morning at Klein's home near New Fane. Klein had placed some dynamite in the oven of the kitchen stove to dry it out and was just opening the oven door to remove it when it exploded. Klein's face was literally blown to pieces, both eyes being blown out and he was also terribly injured otherwise. Miss Theresa Schultz, daughter of Peter Schultz, who also lives on the Klein place, was blown through the door of the building, while her brother was blown through a window by the force of the explosion. Both were injured although not seriously.

Marihuana Found In City Is Destroyed By Police Today

The first patch of marihuana weed to be discovered growing in this city was destroyed this morning by police officials.

Chief Walter H. Wagner withheld the location of the patch "for the good of the community." He said he feared there might be a few roots left and that "it is best that no one knows where it is."

Police are investigating to determine whether the dangerous weed, also known as "Indian hemp," "hashish" and "loco weed," was growing wild or whether it was being cultivated.

A drive on marihuana was started a week ago by Milwaukee county authorities. More than 100 patches have been found in that county since that time. Sunday a large growth of the weed was destroyed by Sheriff Joseph J. Dreps south of Waldo.

For many years the fibers of the male plant were used in Wisconsin for the manufacture of hemp and twine. The seeds are often used to feed pet canaries. About 10 years ago the use of the leaves and blossoms for cigarettes was introduced into the United States by Mexicans.

The drug is a growing menace in this country, especially among young people. Its use frequently leads to violent crimes, illness and eventually insanity.

September 1938

Oakland Tribune Oakland - California - November 22, 1907
Hair On His Plate Sends Him On Rampage

Sheboygan, Wis. - Because he found hair on his plate at breakfast, Frank Demann, a real estate dealer and contractor, smashed the plate, broke up the dining room furniture, and beat his wife. He was arrested and fined $14.

The difference between genius and stupidity
is that genius has its limits.

Unknown

It is better to be coward for a minute
than to be dead for the rest of your life.

Old Irish Proverb

Here Are Few Rules For Those Who Enjoy Drinking

By WM. F. SULLIVAN
(United Press Staff Correspondent)

Chicago, (UP) — You fellows — and girls — who like wines and beers, just keep on drinking; it's a pleasant way to get needed water into the system.

"Some people can't take it," Dr. Gustav Egloff said in an interview today, "and that is one of the reasons we had the prohibition amendment. Because their systems could not take alcoholic beverages, they thought it was wrong morally."

Dr. Egloff, president of the Chicago Chemists' club, who is attending the sessions of the American Chemical society, laid down a few rules for drinkers.

Beneficial To Body

"Drinking in moderation for those who like it," he said, "is a golden rule. Some people don't like water. By and large, light wines and beer are beneficial to the body. It is an easy and pleasant way of getting needed water into the system.

"Most humans are moderate and as a matter of fact before the prohibition amendment was enacted, imbibing of alcoholic beverages was dwindling. When the amendment is repealed, we will come back to non-poisonous beverages, properly fermented under natural conditions, instead of having to rely on bootleggers and the criminals who surround them."

On the question of hard liquors and as to the number of drinks one can take safely, Dr. Egloff said that was an individual's own problem to decide.

Each Affected Differently

"A man who hasn't had a drink in six months," he explained, "might feel sharply the effects of a couple of drinks. The highest stimulation from alcohol comes by drinking before meals — on an empty stomach. One individual might feel a couple of glasses of beer while another could take eight with little effect."

Alcohol, he said, has been with man from time immemorial and the human body has inured itself, grown and developed through countless centuries by the extraordinary vintages which man through his skill, has made.

Dr. Egloff also had a suggestion for the heavy, hard-liquor drinker who wakens in the morning with what is known as a bad "hang-over."

"Some people after excessive drinking," he explained, "are in a semi-coma or stupidness for a week. It might be wise for that type to taper off and not break off sharply or the reaction would be too great. To others second-day drinking is repugnant. Again it is the individual's case to work out."

NATION WILL BE BONE DRY AFTER JULY 1ST, 1919; WILSON SIGNS

Must Designate Brand Of Beer

Madison Wis —(AP)— Dispensers of beer in Wisconsin will be required to display a sign on or near each tap or faucet disclosing the brand of beer drawn under provisions of a bill signed yesterday by Governor La Follette

Sheboygan Press—
August 28, 1935

Sheboygan Press—July 19, 1927

State Dry Men Fined As Drunks

Menominee, Mich. — D. W. Babcock and W. J. Owners, Wisconsin state prohibition agents, were fined $39.90 and $22.90 in Marinette, Wis., justice court Monday on pleading guilty to drunk and disorderly charges. The agents declared they had obtained more "evidence" than they could carry.

PRESENT-DAY FILLING STATIONS

We now have two kinds of filling stations, one kind dispensing liquor and the other, gasoline. Both kinds contribute generously to joy-riding. Until the automobile came into general use, the liquor-dispensing stations, from the beginning of the civilization (?) of the country, monopolized the filling-up of its inhabitants, and they are holding their own very well, even in the keen competition of the "gas" stations, which came with the automobiles.

But the liquor-dispensing stations of earlier times were of quite a different type than they are now. Most of them were in pre-prohibition times conducted in a legitimate, orderly manner, were patronized by men only, women, boys and girls not being permitted to frequent them, and their operators were mostly respectable persons, who suffered no lowering of social standing thru their business. Indeed, some of them were held in high esteem and were considered very desirable citizens, who never attempted to evade the stiff license tax imposed on their business.

Contrasting the old-time saloon-keepers with the ones who today operate our many speakeasies and roadhouses (by courtesy called drink parlors!), the latter we find today are far below the social standing of the former, and justly so, when we realize how they conduct their establishments, dispensing synthetic drinks to all—men, women and children—who come there and ask for them.

Women, girls and boys were not permitted by law to frequent the old-time saloons, and if they did so, they were not considered respectable, while now all are welcome there who have the price and care nothing for loss of social standing. Many of the roadhouses are cloaks for brothels, and they are also patronized by young boys and girls, the boys getting their hip-flasks filled with vile liquor, and leaving the roadhouses after filling up well there, and traveling in automobiles with their girlies, many of the latter starting on their way to lasting grief in this manner.

And still prohibition is persistently called a noble experiment—in Washington, D. C.

"Ve get so soon oldt und yet so late schmardt Better VE TAKE ONE"

Rules That Beer Is Intoxicating

Madison, Wis. —(AP)— Attorney General John Martin ruled today that beer is an intoxicating liquor in the meaning of the drunken driving statute.

In reply to an inquiry from J. Kyle Anderson, district attorney of Waupaca county, Martin said that the supreme court had held it would take judicial notice that beer is intoxicating.

"If the offender was intoxicated in fact, that should be sufficient proof that what he drank was intoxicating," Martin said.

business   Teeth extracted 50c   Dr Rose.

BEER AND LIGHT WINE MUST RETURN

Every fair minded citizen demands that beer and light wine for the home, legally made and sold under government restrictions, will eliminate the violators who are now manufacturing illegally various killing concoctions of unknown proportionate contents made in homes or brought into homes from homes elsewhere. It will bring beneficial beverage in place of the present deadly doses of positive poison. Those who do not care to drink need not. Those who wish to can. Those who wish to will anyhow. Then let science serve them and save them from sure suicide. Beers and light wines manufactured by scientists and sold under government restrictions will build a stronger nation and will satisfy human nature and human appetite.

Men and women who reasonably drank only beer before, deprived of that now, are sinking to the vicious, distilled alcohols that are procurable. You surely are willing to have light wine and beer brought to you in a legal and legitimate way instead of home brew, moonshine, and other poisonous concoctions that are destroying the flower of the human race. Therefore, become a supporting member by sending in by mail or bringing personally to R. H. Baumann, treasurer, Bank of Sheboygan, $1 00 and filling out the attached membership blank today.

Join with this membership blank and $1 NOW.
Sign, Clip Out, and Mail, At Once.

R. A. BAUMANN, TREAS.,
   Bank of Sheboygan,
      Sheboygan, Wis.

Enclosed find one dollar and my membership to Wisconsin Branch, the Association Against the Prohibition Amendment.

Name ....

Address ....

MAY

Are you beginning to feel the lagging spring feeling that makes you tired all day? The best remedy for that is

SCHREIER'S BEER

Makes You Feel Gay in the Month of May

THE KONRAD SCHREIER COMPANY

KINGSBURY
— PALE —

Is a Malt Beverage just filled with important body-building elements.

Rich in food value—it is good for both young and old.

Brewed, aged and bottled by

Gutsch Products Co.

LABOR RENEWS BEER DEMANDS

The Sheboygan Press

VOL. XXIV, NO. 253   SHEBOYGAN, WIS., THURSDAY, OCTOBER 15, 1931   PRICE 3 CENTS

Wednesday's Circulation
17,340

Defense Rests In Trial Of Capone

List Race Losses At $375,000

Japanese Government Submits To U. S. Intervention

Seek Legalization Of 2.75 Per Cent Beer

Re-Elected

Mistrial Ruled

State Tax Omitted On Property

Communities To Gain Benefit Of Large Balance In General Fund Of State

Ready To Lead Armies

Change In Attitude Is Evidenced

League Council Acts After Prevailing Upon Japan Not To Raise Objection

---

When wages are cut the standards of living are lowered. Admitting that the Steel corporations have suffered along with the rest of the country, where is there any justification for the lowering of wages? If business does not warrant the present schedule of hours, reduce the hours but not the wage scale. If these corporations will reduce the salary and bonus payments of the higher-ups, the toilers will not be forced to submit to less than a living wage. When wages are cut the buying power of the masses is reduced and depressions are forced over a greater area for an increased period. Let us as real Americans condemn every step which is taken in the interest of wage reductions, tending as they do to deny the rising generation a fair and fighting chance for some of the advantages which the favored enjoy. If this step is followed throughout the nation it would result in denying to the future citizenship hope of attaining a living wage.—Editor Sheboygan Press.

The Sheboygan Press

Wednesday's Circulation
17,253

VOL. XXIV, No. 237   SHEBOYGAN, WIS., THURSDAY, SEPTEMBER 24, 1931   PRICE 3 CENTS

LEGION DENOUNCES PROHIBITION

War Heroes Vote Against Dry Law By 1,008 To 394

"We Want Beer"

Slays Woman On Farm Near Eau Claire

Bonus Plan Is Rejected By Legion

Minority Report For Paying Certificates At Face Value Is Lost 502 To 982

To Get Facts

Hyde Will Study Beer Proposals

Agriculture Secretary Seeks Information On Economic Aspects Of Question

Bright Spots Appear On Industrial Horizon

Assailant Then Ends Own Life

Authorities Unable To Discover Motive Of Slaying On Farm Of Young Couple

EXTRA!

Paramount Men Named In Warrant

Depression Analyzed

End of Prohibition at Olive's Bar — 11th Street and Michigan Avenue
(420-369)

End of Prohibition 1933 - Adolph Hingiss, Mayor

Subterranean Grain Fields Resulting from "Moon" Mash Cause Sewers To Be Clogged

Sheboygan Press—June 13, 1924

Will the moonshine traffic in Sheboygan make it necessary for the city to plan a special disposal system to carry away the waste of that contraband product? It begins to look that way according to City Engineer C. U. Boley, who says that his department is continually confronted with the problem of opening up the sewers after they have been clogged with deposits of mash and subterranean grain fields that result. If a new drainage system, built especially for the purpose of carrying away refuse of an illicit business becomes necessary, then who would be compelled to pay for it? ...

Something Must Be Done

The condition is continually growing worse, according to Mr. Boley, and it is costing the city large sums of money to remedy it. If the moonshiner is honest or has any conscience, here is an idea that may suit: Realizing that there is a great deal of extra cost in cleaning mash-clogged sewers, he might be willing to cast his mite occasionally into what could be called a Conscience Box, which could be installed on some inconspicuous corner. The Conscience Box could be designed on the order of a strong box or safe, so that it would be impossible for burglars to break into it and steal its contents, and a special city officer could be designated to go the rounds several times each night to make collections.

Here the moonshiner who is fortunate to escape the law, might drop in a certain small—it would necessarily be small, very small—percentage of the profits he makes on his product, that the city may be re-imbursed to a slight extent for the extra labor and expense incurred in cleaning the sewers of their masses of foots, solid filth and growing plants that result from the bash being thrown into them because of the conveniences of modern times, and because this method of disposal destroys evidence, thus making arrest and conviction less probable.

Just recently, according to Mr. Boley, the city street crew struck one of the worst spots encountered since people started making their own, as well as a lot for others. Two blocks of sewer some place between N. Eighth street and N. Twelfth street on Michigan Avenue was so solidly packed with mash, growing corn and other root formations, that it was extremely difficult for city laborers to force a steel cable through. They had to get the cable from one manhole to another so they could pull a sewer cleaning machine after it. After much effort, they managed to get it through. Then, they drew through it a turbine engine equipped with revolving knives, and freed the conduit of its overload. ...

Sheboygan Press—June 7, 1921

Moonshine Egg Latest

[By United Press]

Madison, Wis. — The moonshine egg has made its appearance in Madison. It has baffled both the police and the prohibition enforcement agents. The bootlegger inventing the deception told his secret only after going out of business.

He blew out the contents of hens eggs, he said and then filled the shells with liquor. Sealing wax was applied to repair the broken portions of the shells and make them liquor tight. The shells were placed in a large market basket and kept in plain view.

Evidence came to the authorities that the Madison man was selling liquor by the drink at his home and a series of raids were ordered. Eight times within six weeks officers visited the home, each time making a thorough search liquor was never found, even though spotters had reported to the officials that they had purchased there. An egg shell holds about three fingers of liquor, the bootlegger said.

PITCHED HAY TO UNCOVER JUGS OF MOONSHINE

Sheboygan Press—
January 20, 1921

[By Associated Press.]

La Crosse.—Just how hard federal prohibition agents have to work in some cases was indicated in U. S. court here before Judge Landis today when Agent Carl Henning testified he pitched three tons of hay in the barn of Peter Harris, farmer living near Necedah, before uncovering the jugs of moonshine liquor he sought.

Harris was tried today on a charge of having a still, three barrels of raisin mash and seven jugs of moonshine liquor in his possession, and also with selling his product. Guy Wheelihan of Necedah, a telephone lineman, testified he bought five pints of liquor from Harris. Harris admitted owning the still and said he had been making liquor for his own use since 1919 but was not selling his product.

The jury in the case of John Brickler, Park Falls hardware merchant, charged with manufacturing stills without a government permit, returned a verdict of guilty.

At La Crosse, before Judge K. M. Landis, Charles Lum, Milton Junction section hand, was found guilty by a jury, of having in his possession and operating a still in his home.

In this same court John Brickler, who operated a hardware store and repair shop at Park Falls, Price county, was tried on the charge to having in his possession materials for the making of a still and with having made stills without a license.

Joseph Gelinak, a farmer living near Black River Falls, was charged with having a still and a barrel of raisin mash and with selling his liquor to Black River Falls men.

These men were to be sentenced today.

45

Visitors Are Barred From Visiting Blast Scene Near St. Ann

Visitors to the farm of Ed. Ehlenbeck, a mile west of St. Ann and just north of the Sheboygan county line, were barred Thursday afternoon from viewing the ruins of the barn that was burned to the ground in some mysterious manner at 5 p. m., Wednesday, severely burning two men who were in the place at the time, and causing known damage of $1,600.

The estimated damage given does not include the loss on a steam boiler, a huge copper still, coils, pipes, tanks, coal, kegs, barrels, and other paraphernalia that was in the barn. It includes Mr. Ehlenbeck's calculation as to the loss he suffered on the barn, which he figured was worth $1,500, and machinery that he had stored in the building, estimated to be worth about $100. Other machinery that Mr. Ehlenbeck had in the barn was removed in time to save it from destruction.

The building that was destroyed by the flames was abandoned as a barn and was used as a machinery shed and for other storing purposes until a month ago, when, according to reports brought back here by two men who inspected the ruin after successfully overcoming the objections of the owner to view the premises, Mr. Ehlenbeck rented the barn to two men whom he said were strangers to him at the time, but who told him they were from Chicago.

Rented a Month

Mr. Ehlenbeck told his Thursday afternoon visitors, according to their statements on returning to Sheboygan, that rented the barn a little over a month ago to men who gave the names of Gordon Spangel and Armin Luecke. These names, however, do not correspond with those given for publication in Thursday's Press. The names reported yesterday were Arthur Tennant and E. C. Luecke. They paid him in advance for the use of the building, he is reported to have said.

The Ehlenbeck farm is a combination of two former farms and has a total area of 160 acres. It formerly had two barns and two houses. The owner is occupying the house and using the barn within view of the county line road, but the other is hidden from the road view by a grove of trees on a hill northwest of the main buildings. It is reached by a road that winds around the hill through the Ehlenbeck farm yard.

When two Sheboygan men went out to inspect the destroyed property yesterday, they were given a frigid greeting by Mr. Ehlenbeck, who had been doing some work in his barn. They asked to view the ruins, but were informed that Spangel and Luecke had given him strict orders to refuse everyone that privilege. Asked as to the whereabouts of the two men who had been operating the place, he said that they were badly burned and he believed they were in a hospital somewhere. He was not certain where they could be found, but declared that they had rented rooms in St. Ann, and could possibly be found there, although he thought they were not in condition to be interviewed in regard to the manner in which the barn caught fire.

Interview Refused

Statements of Mr. Ehlenbeck in regard to the seriousness of the con-

(Continued on Page 6)

(Continued from page 1.)

ditions of Spangel and Luecke were borne out when those who went out with the idea of questioning them learned at the general store and hotel in St. Ann that, although the men in question were there, they could not be seen.

The visitors "dropped into" the soft drink parlor in the building where the men were reported to have been. There they found a woman behind the bar and they asked for a drink of beer. They were informed that no beer was sold there, but that some near beer or pop could be had. An order was given for the near beer after which the callers left.

Not knowing that Spangel and Luecke were in the same building at the time (or reported to have been there), the enquiring Sheboygan men went to the St. Ann office of Dr. Fechter, who attended the burns of the pair who had rented the barn. Here they were informed by a woman that Dr. Fechter was at his office in Marytown, and would not be back until evening. She stated that at least one of the injured men was stopping at the hotel.

Returning to the hotel the visitors entered by way of the grocery store and here they found the same woman who had previously waited upon them in the bar room. She was attending to the wants of customers at the grocery counter when she was asked whether the man who was burned could be seen. She declared that he was resting and must not be disturbed. Another woman who said she and other relatives had gone all the way to St. Ann (from where she did not say) to see the fire victims, emphasized the fact that the one in question would not be seen as he was under the doctor's care, giving the impression thereby that he was in serious condition and could not have visitors, especially those whom he did not desire to see.

"Is the other man here," one of the enquirers asked. Still another woman stepped from a hallway off the grocery store and soft drink parlor and exclaimed indignantly, "Yes, that man is my husband, and nobody is going to see him." With these greetings, salutations and cutting glances the visitors were given

to understand that their company was no longer desired. Not wishing to disobey the orders of the attending physician in view of the fact that by doing so they might add to the seriousness of the men's conditions, they departed on their way to Sheboygan.

Reported Explosion

It was reported yesterday that the destructive blaze was caused by the explosion of a 250-gallon copper still which had probably been used in manufacturing something that might cause an explosion under given conditions. Whether this was true or not, the remains of what was undoubtedly a still and all the equipment to go with it was observed in a ruined mass in what had been the basement of the barn, according to the report brought back here.

The stone foundation of a barn approximately 80 to 40 feet in dimensions and the concrete silo walls were all that withstood the ravages of the raging flames that destroyed the lumber part of the structure and the part of its contents that could not be removed.

At the notheast corner of the barn stood the silo, and at the bottom of this was a large steam boiler. A pile of burning coal strongly indicated that the boiler had been in use quite recently. The smoke stack of the boiler was concealed within the silo, and the smoke escaped through windows of the silo, judging from the coal soot around the windows. Portions of the still, twisted and broken coils and pipes were seen at various places on the ground where the floor had been before the fire. At the south side of the barn beside the wall was a long concrete tank divided into sections, which would have been suitable as mash tanks.

The layout in the barn was such as to make an ideal combination for the manufacture of illicit liquor, if anyone had had a mind to go into that business.

Trench From Windmill

A windmill stands a short distance northwest of the west end of the barn. A trench led from the windmill to the barn, but pipes had not been laid in the trench up to yesterday afternoon, according to reports made by the two unwelcome visitors. Another trench had been dug for a short distance from the east end of the barn toward down an incline. "It would not be difficult to imagine," one of the visitors said upon his return, "what those trenches were for, although Mr.

Ehlenbeck told them that he had paid little attention to what was going on at this particular property because he had rented it.

Volunteer Firemen Called

Mr. Ehlenbeck said that when the fire occurred, volunteer fire departments from St. Ann and St. Cloud were called out, and they did all they could, but failed to save the building and a portion of its contents.

It was a long time before the visitors could persuade Mr. Ehlenbeck to permit their visiting the barn. He stated that earlier visitors had torn up his clover field, and that, besides, his renters had forbidden him to let anyone on the farm. He finally led the way around the south side of the hill through a pasture and around the edge of a clover field, entailing the necessity of crawling through gates and fences.

Mr. Ehlenbeck said he was under the impression that the road leading to the destroyed barn was impassable. The walk back was by way of the road, which proved to be much shorter and easier for walking.

Asked whether Mr. Spangel and Mr. Luecke had been manufacturing liquor in the barn, Mr. Ehlenbeck said that they had not finished any, that they had just started to operate their still Wednesday afternoon, according to the story related by the Sheboygan men on their return to this city. He is reported to have said they had been making beer before that. The set-up indicated that conditions would have been suitable for such work.

Mr. Ehlenbeck had been on his present farm for about a year, having traded a farm near Rockville for it.

This photograph shows the ruins of a barn on a farm owned by Ed. Ehlenbeck resulting from a fire and the explosion of a still. The stone foundation of the barn, approximately 80 by 40 feet in dimensions and the concrete silo walls were all that withstood the ravages of the raging flames.

Grade of Drunkenness

The boisterous loud voice of the drunkard usually comes not from a desire to be loud and domineering, as seems, but from a very different and simple cause. The nerve of hearing is quickly affected by alcohol, so the poor chap is sillily shouting only to hear himself talk, for he is slightly "drunken deaf." "Dead drunk" is not only more euphonious, but is a truer description than "blind drunk." — New York Press.

"Thank God, the country has gone dry. It will bring sunshine to many a home!" said the speaker.

"Yes, and moonshine too, brother." answered the skeptic.

What Every Wife Should Say To Her Husband

Here is no sentimentalizing about the "drink" question: no moralizing: not the story of a drunkard's wife or the wife of a man who "drinks." It is the ringing word of the wife of an "average" man, of seven out of every ten men. What this woman says, how she says it, what should be "on the lips of every wife and every woman," should be read by every wife, mother or woman. It is a clear, true, ringing note on a much-muddled question.

In the June

LADIES' HOME JOURNAL

15 Cents a Copy, of All News Agents, or $1.50 a Year by Mail Direct or Through Any Authorized Subscription Agent. On Sale Now by All Newsdealers

Our Distributing Agent is

SELSMEYER & FISCHER
809 North 8th Street   *Sheboygan, Wis.*

THE CURTIS PUBLISHING COMPANY
Independence Square, Philadelphia, Pennsylvania

THE END OF PROHIBITION

While Milwaukee waited until Lent was finished, a river of beer flowed through Sheboygan at 12:01 a.m., April 7, 1933, the first possible minute it was legal to again sell beer. Leading up to Prohibition, surveys in county newspapers showed that ten to one, people were in favor of changing the Dry Laws. This was strongly opposite to national opinion. President Roosevelt, legalizing the sale of 3.2 beer, had modified the Volstead Act. This was done in part because it would raise tax revenue. Charles Broughton, Editor of the Sheboygan Press, received the first case of Kingsbury off the line because of his strong appeals for the end of Prohibition. Reports in the Sheboygan Press told of a variety of problems unique to Prohibition. Raids by Federal Agents were common to Sheboygan, with establishments such as Yankee Hill, the Hemlock Inn, the Labor Buffet, and the Midget Café all receiving government attention. Herman Eisold was raided only nine days after he bought his brother's business. Christmas in 1917, the last one before Prohibition, saw two Drunk and Disorderly arrests. During the Christmas of 1927, thirteen citations were handed out. Mrs. Kardas filed charges against her husband, Stanley, after he sold her bicycle to buy moonshine. Apparently moonshine in Sheboygan was stronger than that served elsewhere. Peter DeGroot blamed the liquor's potency for selling his farm at a greatly reduced price. Steve Kotowski, of Milwaukee, blamed his activity on Sheboygan moonshine, which was stronger than what he was used to. The Judge agreed with him and gave him a lesser fine.

Return of 3.2 Beer. This photo shows a celebration, involving three cases of Gutsch Beer and a German Band, at the home of Sheboygan Press publisher, Charles Broughton. The celebration took place on April 7, 1933 and was inspired by the end of Prohibition and the return of 3.2% beer.

Prohibition in the United States was a measure designed to reduce drinking by eliminating the businesses that manufactured, distributed, and sold alcoholic beverages. The Eighteenth Amendment to the U.S. Constitution took away license to do business from the brewers, distillers, vintners, and the wholesale and retail sellers of alcoholic beverages. The leaders of the prohibition movement were alarmed at the drinking behavior of Americans, and they were concerned that there was a culture of drink among some sectors of the population that, with continuing immigration from Europe, was spreading.

In the spring of 1933, Franklin D. Roosevelt made "real beer" exempt from the 18th amendment. By December of the same year, Utah was last necessary state to ratify the 21st amendment -- repeal of prohibition -- and on December 5th, alcohol was legal once more.

Lame, Halt And The Blind Go To Millhome For Herb Cures Of 83-Year-Old Eccentric Healer

Sheboygan Press—, March 11, 1927

Go to Harbrecht at Millhome. That is what the word passed from lips to lips of sufferers from miles around who futilely have tried to overcome the pains of disorders and who are making supreme efforts once more to win back health. Harbrecht's shanty at Millhome, a little settlement a few miles from Kiel, is sought each day by a dozen, sometimes many more, patients who hold out a ray of hope that this 83-year-old eccentric will be able to cure with his herb medicine and strange treatments all kinds of ailments with which they are afflicted. No one seems to doubt his power to cure them. Gladly they take home with them a little bottle of herb medicine or a box of pills which he prepares in his little stock room. His orders to come back after thirty days are obeyed without question. John J. Harbrecht is very likable, but at the same time he is very independent. When interviewed he wanted to talk in German, and when the reporter said he could not understand that language, Harbrecht told him to go home and study it. Harbrecht said he can understand thirty languages and can speak sixteen of them fluently. It is difficult to get a definite statement from Harbrecht. Upon questioning, he replied that he comes from Russian stock and that he lived among Indian tribes for many years. ... Surely some of his knowledge of the medicinal qualities of herbs was gained from the Indians. His barn is full of herbs. More herbs are mixed with the debris, the accumulation of household effects in his shanty... The healer once was a blacksmith. He also was a veterinary. Sketches, many of them of a humorous character, which he showed during the interview, indicate that he is an artist of no mean ability. He is a cook.

How does Harbrecht go about his business of healing the sick? The first thing he does is take a blood test by vigorously rubbing a patient's skin where the blood is near the surface. With a magnifying glass he examines the red spot made by this rubbing and from that ascertains the condition of the blood. Harbrecht after making a blood test, will look a patient in the eye and immediately tell him what the ailment is.

After this story ran, the Wisconsin Board of Medical Examiners visited Harbrecht, and needless to say, it did not go well for the healer. He was warned to discontinue his practice due to a slew of violations. Practicing medicine without a license or a certificate of registration from the state board was among his greatest offense. The inspector, William Krause, was quoted as saying "Harbrecht's home is nothing more than a refuse pile attached to an abandoned blacksmith shop. In the room where he treats his patients there is an old bed covered with blankets which in my opinion have never been washed. All the patients sit on the same blanket, no matter what disease is afflicting them." The investigation was thought necessary due to a peaked interest in the "doctor."

Despite Harbrecht's outlandish,

vague description of himself his marriage license gives slightly different information. John C. F. Harbrecht was the son of John J. D. and Dorothea Harbrecht in Klinken, Grand Dukedom Mecklinberg, Schwerin on February 4, 1854. He married Charlotta DeForth in the town of Rhine on January 19, 1880. The couple had eight children. Harbrecht died April 4, 1940 at his home in Plymouth and is buried in Rockville Cemetery in Manitowoc County.

Was Harbrecht a quack? Maybe, although his 'medicine' seems to have cured a lot of people who believed in him.

Bruehl
1910 Cpd

"Man Sitting on Dead Horse" — A 143-Year Old Sheboygan County Mystery

This man and this horse have been part of an ongoing 'investigation' for the better part of seven years. Initially not much was known about the unique pair. What we do know is that the scene is Griffith Street, which later became Eighth Street, and Indiana Avenue in Sheboygan, looking north toward the Eighth Street bridge. The bridge was built in 1865. A saloon, the building to the right, on the north east corner of the intersection, was the Lakeview House, later called the Evergreen City Hotel. The wooden buildings north of the Lakeview House are part of the C. Reiss & Co. yards. To the left of the bridge and across the river is the Michael Winter Lumber Company.

Now to the more pressing questions: Why is this man in the top hat sitting on this horse? Who is this man? Is the horse really dead?

It has been suggested that it could have been staged for a political campaign ad of some sort. "Based on the time period, the well-dressed man sitting on the horse and the apparent 'staging' of the photo it might be fruitful to check into persons who had run for offices during that time period." Another suggestion offered was "One of the solutions, back then, for severe equine gaseous emissions, was to assist the animal in expelling the excess flatulence. This was accomplished by unharnessing the animal, having it lie down on its side, with the animals hindquarters pointed downwind, if, hopefully, there was some, and then vigorously bouncing up and down on the animal until the sound of horse farting is about one second in duration per bounce.

Another speculation was that it was a trick horse and it was not dead at all. Perhaps they were part of a small circus or sideshow that was visiting the area. Maybe the man was trying to sell his "famous horse elixir that calms the most nervous horses?" Steven Long, editor of Texas Horse Talk magazine, weighed in with the possibility that the horse was in the middle of a training session. Long stated "It's real common practice among trainers — laying a horse down. It teaches calmness, teaches trust. And they'll sit on the horse. Very frequently, they'll have their photograph taken and I have no doubt this could have happened." The lack of tack secured this notion for some other people.

Some of us are convinced the horse is indeed dead. Some people suggested that the horse is not stiff so it couldn't possibly be dead. However, rigor mortis sets in at around four hours in horses; perhaps this photo was taken soon after the horse perished. As for why the man didn't leave his horse lie and go about his business, we can look to a city ordinance for the answer. In 1867 the Common Council passed the first traffic regulations and they state any "unsound beef, pork, fish, hides or skins of any kind found within the city... must be destroyed or buried." There was a fine ($25.00 in the 1870s, $750 today) to the person who left their deceased animal on the street, so perhaps this gentleman was waiting for the 'undertaker' to come take his horse.

There were only a few photographers in Sheboygan at the time of this photo — David Hawkins, W. Morgenmeier, Harmon and Manville and Groh. Any of them could have taken the photograph. Any of them could be the photographed.

The speculation of who this man is has been so much fun. Whether we'll ever know who he really is a long shot but until then, here are four of our front runners.

Louis Roenitz

George M. Groh

James Jackson

Frank Roenitz

A Dead Horse of a Different Color

by Colleen Fitzpatrick and Andrew Yeiser

It doesn't take a rocket scientist —- or maybe it does.

The excitement over the Dead Horse picture ... produced much speculation on who the man in the top hat and tails was and why he was photographed sitting on a dead horse in the middle of S. 8th St. in Sheboygan, WI. But it took a couple rocket scientists, Colleen Fitzpatrick and Andrew Yeiser, to nail down when and how the photograph was taken. Colleen and Andy are optical scientists, and experts in analyzing old photographs. ... With the help of historical map expert Sharon Sergeant of Ancestral Manor, along with a bit of Sheboygan history provided by the Sheboygan County Historical Research Center, they found the photograph was taken on September 24, 1871 at 4:30 pm.

How did they do it? Elementary, my dear Watson.

All speculation aside, the direction and height of the shadows were the most important to the "when" of the photograph. All the shadows in the picture-those of Mr. Top-Hat-and-Tails, his dead horse, the buildings, and the man with the dog—stretch directly across the street. Since S. 8th St. (then Griffith St.) runs north-south, the shadows point almost exactly east-west. There are only two days in the year when this occurs, the Spring Equinox (March 19-20) and the Fall Equinox (September 22-23). ...Considering a top hat and tails are not appropriate attire for Sheboygan in March when the average temperature is about 32°F, the date of the picture must have been September 22-23.

What about the time of day? Mr. Dapper is not only holding down his dead horse, he is also acting as a sundial. By measuring the length of his shadow on the street, Colleen and Andy were able to calculate the angle of the sun in the sky. This told them the photo was taken at 4:30 p.m.

What is the earliest date this picture could have been taken? This is where being an optical scientist come s in handy. Andy observed that the photograph was snapped using a wide angle lens. How did he know this? For one thing, the width of the street was 80 ft. To take in half of the street using a normal lens, the camera would have been about 80 ft. from the horse. But this is clearly not where the camera was. A wide angle lens explains the discrepancy.

The rest of "A Dead Horse of a Different Color" is available at the SCHRC.

Mrs. Helen B. Cole, Sole Surviving Wisconsin Civil War Nurse

LaCrosse Tribune & Leader-Press—June 15, 1931

Encampment, Recalls Death of Lincoln Experiences As War Nurse Are Related

Mrs. Helen B. Cole, Sheboygan, sole surviving Wisconsin nurse of Civil war days, recounted a personal battlefield experience Monday which makes patriotism everlasting.

The woman, intimate of Abraham Lincoln, Clara Barton, Red Cross founder, all Union army generals, is 93 years young, appears to be but 50. She decries prohibition, liquor abuses.

She passed through death stricken areas, sentiment shattered homes, and emerged unscathed by warfare's ravages. But let her tell the story as she did in the Hotel Stoddard Monday morning.

"After the Battle of the Wilderness I was in a tent taking dictation from a dying captain writing a farewell letter to his sweetheart in Maine.

President Lincoln Enters

"A little drummer boy, on a nearby cot, throat wounded, lay shivering. I stepped over to him , covered him with a large flag. Just then Abraham Lincoln, president of the United States, came in.

He walked to the cot. 'Why my little man, you did not have to go to war,' Mr. Lincoln said. 'Aren't you sorry you came?'

"The boy, vocal cords impaired, talked with great effort. He managed to say, while stroking the flag atop him, 'Why no, if I had 100 loves to give, I would give them all to this flag.'

"Mr. Lincoln was called away for a brief meeting. He returned but in the meantime the drummer boy had died and his body had been removed. Mr. Lincoln went to where the body was, caught it up in his arms, kissed that dead boy's face. " 'Oh God,' prayed Lincoln as tears streamed down his face. Oh God, please make me as true to this flag as this little drummer man was loyal'."

Silence followed the recitation. No one dared interrupt Mrs. Cole's thoughts. A moment later she continued.

Will Never Forget

"I will never forget when Mr. Lincoln was assassinated. I knew the family immediately. It was just after Willie Lincoln died and I was nursing Tad back to health. Tad was crying. He suddenly turned to me and said, "Oh nurse, I miss my pa so. You know if Pa was alive today he would forgive the man who killed him"

Two women in the room wiped tears from their eyes. Mrs. Cole's eyes were watery, but her voice was far from choking.

"Anybody who says women were not respected by Union soldiers in the Civil war, lies. I was a nurse. I knew many nurses. We went to the war in those days as a mother, sister, wife, sweetheart, companion, friend of the soldier. No army nurse I know of was ever insulted by the men. Clara Barton and I slept together several times beneath wagons, we got lice and insects all over our bodies. We went through hardships. But we never were insulted by men."

No Anesthetics

"Another thing. In that war there was no anesthetics to use nor no X-ray machines. Doctors just probed for the bullet balls. We only had real brandy and good whiskey to ease pain. The greatest crime ever perpetrated in this country was the passage of prohibition measures. Liquor, rightly used and not abused, is a Godsend. It is needed, and I oppose liquor prohibition."

Sheboygan Press — June 15, 1925

Mrs. Cole sat at the same table with John Wilkes Booth at a game of whist just three weeks before the assassination. (Whist is an English trick taking card game played by four people.) In later years through friends, Mrs. Cole received an invitation to the wedding of the daughter of Edwin Booth, the brother of the assassinator, and the famous Shakespearean actor. After the wedding Mr. Booth called Mrs. Cole into his library and asked her a few questions about his brother. He shook his head and said nothing when Mrs. Cole answered him.

After the war Mrs. Cole was sent to Memphis, Tenn., to close a hospital for colored veterans. The scene of her life shifted to Boston after she had accomplished her task in Memphis, and it was here that she spent the majority of her years prior to returning to Sheboygan Falls.

July 8, 1911

CUPID IS BAFFLED IN SHEBOYGAN

Otto Dieckmann a farmer of this county, a widower forty-three years old with seven children wants to get married to Lottie Sturdevant, a county charge living in this city twenty-one years old.

Dieckman says he loves the girl dearly and she blushingly confesses she is enamoured of him. He met Lottie Saturday for the first time and it was love at first sight. She saw Dieckmann for the first time last Saturday and her very soul went out to him. The attraction was mutual so it was decided to apply for a marriage license without any delay.

The application was made yesterday. The course of true love never runs smooth however. The first obstacle was on hand. County Clerk Fischer refused to grant a license. Mr. Dieckmann argued but it was of no avail. Finally with great reluctance the applicant left the office. The County Clerk says that if he had not interfered the Humane Aagent would have. Whether Cupid will win out in this encounter is the question that is the subject of discussion among the friends and neighbors of the parties concerned.

Sheboygan Press —
November 18, 1936

Life Begins At 40?

Mochechi Ntgakele, a Zulu aged 110 years, has just been married again at Harrismith, South Africa. [A fellow with a name like that is liable to do anything.]

I LOVE HIM ALMOST TO DEATH

BEGS MARRIAGE LICENSE

Lottie Sturdevant Tries to Persuade County Clerk to Grant Her a License---Love at First Sight.

"Oh, please Mr. Fischer give me a marriage license, I love him so. If you would only know how r-e-a-l much I love him you would not tell me no. And your father was such a nice—such a good man. And you are such a nice man too. I know you will not say no—because I love him pretty near to death, and he loves me too. Yes, I was introduced to him and I loved him right away—and he did me too. It was love at first sight and we can't get along without each other. Now, Mr. Fischer you will not say no — you are such a good man, such a nice man."

Dressed up in all her Sunday fineries, and beaming on the county clerk with a smile that would make Venus jealous, Lottie Sturdevant, appealed to the county clerk in her sweetest tones attempting to move his heart and grant her a marriage license. Mr. Fischer, leaning back in his large arm chair calmly and unmoved questioned the girl as to what means of support she had had up to that time. She said she had once upon a time worked in the glove shop but at the present time wasn't doing anything and was supported by the county to some extent.

Lottie wants to marry the man she loves. She met him about July 1 and her fascination was so great that three days after he applied to the county clerk for a marriage license. Lottie is only twenty-one years old, but swears by all that is sacred that he is her only love. Her Romeo is 43 years old. He has a large farm near Moome. He was married once before and has seven children. But even that does not affect the ardour of either his or her love. He appealed to the county clerk for a license about two weeks ago and was refused. Lottie however was not so easily satisfied. She must go to the county clerk and try her persuasive powers. So there she went with her mother this morning. A good sized audience was there while she delivered her plea. Mr. Fischer asked her how she thought she would be able to support and raise so large a family when she could not support herself. She said the farm would bring in some money. Finally he told her to call again in the near future, and she left the office half sobbing, affirming that she would become Mrs. Otto Dieckmann even though all the fates were against her. The course of true love never runs smooth, Lottie.

July 25, 1911

SHEBOYGAN PRESS (SHEBOYGAN, WISCONSIN)

61

Three Lakes Man, Age 74, Is Advertising For Wife

Rhinelander, Wis.—(AP)—"Wanted—A wife. Must be between 40 and 65 years of age, sound of wind and limb, and of cheerful nature. I have comfortable home to offer and am eligible for old-age pension. See or write Ezra Worden, Three Lakes, Wis."

This was the advertisement 74-year-old Ezra Worden wanted to insert in the Rhinelander News' classified columns. Instead, it topped a news column, accompanied by details of just what he wants, and does not want.

Worden said he doesn't want a wife under 40 because a younger woman might be flighty. He didn't enlarge on the 65-year limit, but then there was the "sound of wind and limb" provision.

Despite his 74 years, Worden declared stoutly he is a top-notch workman, citing the fact that he picked 700 bushels of potatoes recently and during the blueberry season garnered 350 quarts of berries.

Worden said his marital record speaks for itself on the matter of fidelity and good nature. He married twice. Both wives died. He lived with the second 37 years.

"Some of the people up my way think I don't mean it when I mention getting married," Worden said. "I'm going to show 'em now that I mean business. Winter's coming on and I've got enough money to get married if the charivaris don't cost too much. I've got a good stove in my place out of Three Lakes and after I get it banked up it'll be plenty snug for the winter. My son 'batches' with me and we get along right well. But after all, there's no use going without a woman when there's so many of them around."

"Wanted — A wife. Must be between 40 and 65 years of age, sound of wind and limb, and off cheerful nature..."

Ezra's Advertising Takes Him Along Road To Altar

Rhinelander, Wis — (AP) —Ezra Worden, the 74-year-old woodsman who wooed by public print, had a marriage license and a prospective bride today.

On Nov. 2 the hardy Ezra will march to the altar with Mrs Maggie Cornwall, an Oneida county widow of 52, who Ezra picked from 411 would-be-brides who answered his "wife wanted' advertisement of Oct. 11.

Being twice a widower and experienced in affairs of the heart, Ezra eliminated competitors one by one before he chose his bride-to-be Some were too young and might be giddy, some were too old and might be cross and sickly—until finally the contest narrowed down to a Milwaukee woman and Mrs. Cornwall, he said.

"The Milwaukee woman looked pretty fair but I couldn't wait for her to come up here, so I went out to see Mrs. Cornwall," he said "Now we got it all fixed up. We got the license."

Besides Ezra, Mrs Cornwell gets, according to Worden's advertised claims, a "good warm stove for the winter, a cabin banked up against the cold, and enough extra money for a good charivari" "And I'm old enough to be eligible for an old age pension," he said

"And that isn't all," he said as he chuckled over his good fortune. "You know some of the women that wrote to me is too young for an oldtimer like me, so my son, Marvin, is corresponding with them He's 36 and never been married, so maybe we'll both get hitched out of this."

Residents Of Three Lakes Present At Ezra's Wedding

Three Lakes, Wis. — (UP) — Ezra Worden, 74, a great lover and philosopher of the farm country, gave his want-ad bride a gentle little hug today and was ready to announce to the world "what a happy boy am I!"

Last night Ezra led his bride, Mrs. Maggie Cornwall, 52, Crescent widow, to the altar. He selected her from 411 women who answered his newspaper advertisement for a wife. Replies came from Florida to Canada.

The altar before which the couple said vows at 7 o'clock last night was rigged up on the porch of the Sunnyside hotel. More than 1,000 spectators, bundled in coats and furs against the 24 degree temperature, watched the ceremony performed by the Rev. N. W. Conkle of Three Lakes Congregational church.

The wedding was attended by all the pomp and din of a county fair. The Three Lakes high school band tooted its best and loudest.

There were shouts of "Atta boy, Ezra," and "You're ok, Maggie" as Ezra kissed his bride and then turned to favor the audience with a coy little jig.

"I'm the happiest guy in the world," he announced, smiling down at the blushing Maggie.

In the crowd gathered to watch the wedding were several of the 411 who "didn't make the grade."

After the ceremony there was a wedding supper at the Sunnyside hotel. A Rhinelander baker donated a huge wedding cake for the occasion.

After that there were several public dances given in Ezra's honor.

But Ezra and Maggie disappeared.

An Outrage!

On Tuesday evening of last week, the house of Mr. Goss, Catholic priest at Cascade, was the scene of a Ku Klux outrage. Mr. Goss had been called out to visit a sick person, and left the house in charge of his mother, an elderly lady, who was acting as his housekeeper. He had been absent but a short time when four unknown persons, masked and blacked up to conceal recognition, entered the dwelling, seized and bound Mrs. Goss to her chair to prevent resistance, and proceeded to ransack the house. Nearly every article of any value belonging to the priest, even to his wearing apparel and bed clothes, was carried off, though strange to say none of the church property, of which there was much of value, in the house, was troubled. Many are of the opinion that the perpetrators of the bold deed were actuated by ill will toward the priest, rather than a desire to possess themselves of his personal effects, though they fail to give the least cause for such ill will.

On Friday night of last week about the hour of midnight, some unknown wretch fired a charge of shot through a window in the residence of Reverend Father Tierney, of Cascade. No person is assigned for the cowardly assault. There were two friends of the Rev. Father from Marytown occupying the apartment, when the window was fired into. That no personal injury was occasioned was evidently no fault of those committing the dastardly outrage.

Double Tragedy at
Bank of Elkhart Lake

The Elkhart Lake bank was the site of tragedy on two occasions. Two suicides took place, the first on October 22, 1918 when "Herman W. Hostman committed the rash deed during the noon hour at Elkhart Lake where he was assisting in the conduct of the Bank of Elkhart Lake in the illness of the cashier Herman Osthoff . . . His lifeless body was found hanging from the rafters."

On September 23, 1920, "despondent over ill health. . . Herman Osthoff, former clerk of the village, took his life with his own hands at 8 o'clock in the morning in the basement of the bank building by shooting himself in the head."

No Easy Task To Survive Both Illness And Cure

By DON REEDER

INDIANAPOLIS (AP) — Know somebody who wants to stop stammering? Try smacking him in the face with a piece of liver.

Got lumbago? Boil an old shoe and drink the residue.

The Indiana Historical Bureau reports these and similar home remedies were common among Indiana citizens of a century ago — and even more recently.

It is a noble tribute to the hardiness of Hoosier pioneers that they survived not only their illnesses but their cures.

W. Edson Richmond and Elva Van Winkle, two Indiana University staff members, went searching for remedies that were a part of Indiana life 100 years ago. Here's the list they compiled:

If somebody with blue gums bites you, rum the bite with some black hen litter, and the biter will lose his teeth.

For a cut, bind a poultice of fresh cow manure.

Asthma — Drink a tea made by boiling a hornets' nest.

Head cold — Take nine whiffs from a dirty sock.

Leg cramps Tie some eel skin around the leg.

Croup — Rub the throat with skunk oil and take a dose of oil.

Inflamed finger joints — Catch a weasel and squeeze it to death.

Goiter — Pass a dead person's hand over the throat.

Headache — Drink a stiff shot of water mixed with wood ashes.

Influenza — Drink hot milk laced with pepper.

Measles — Rub with sheep dung.

Rabies — Burn the bite for at least eight seconds with a red-hot iron.

Rheumatism — Rub the afflicted parts with the blood of a freshly killed rattlesnake.

Not all the cures were so disagreeable. Many ailments — including cholera, fever, lung fever and others — called for a liberal dose of whiskey or gin. That particular remedy undoubtedly went down easier than the hornets' nest tea.

Other pioneer prescriptions fell into the category of "spells" instead of medicine. Like these:

Bleeding — To stop bleeding, pronounce the Biblical verse Ezekiel 16:6 silently three times.

General diseases — Lay on the afflicted part a hair from the head of a man who has never seen his father.

Freckles — Remove them by washing in dew the first of May.

Leg pains — Wear a dime around the ankle on a string.

Corns — Put shaving soap in the shoes.

Chills — Step across a creek backwards.

Rheumatism — Carry a potato or a chestnut in the pocket.

Toothache — To prevent toothaches, trim fingernails only on Fridays.

Warts — Rub the wart with a stolen dishrag and then hide the dishrag in a tree stump.

Sheboygan Press—May 27, 1926

AROUND WISCONSIN

From some of the comments, it would appear that there are people in the country who will not believe that the North Pole has been discovered until they are shown a piece of it.—Oshkosh Daily Northwestern.

Even then they would declare it to be an imitation. Some people are so skeptical that had they lived in the time of Jesus, they would not have loaned him a cent unless he gave them a mortgage on heaven.

This method of execution is novel, bizarre, but apparently no less swift and merciful than other older systems, and it has the merit of eliminating some of the horrid death trappings of other kinds of capital punishment.—Beloit Daily News.

No method of executing human beings could be devised which has anything merciful connected with it, the elimination of some of the barbarous features connected with other forms of capital punishment notwithstanding.

The proposition made by Frank Lloyd Wright that his second wife be paid $1,000 and $125 a month for one year if she would give him a divorce, was turned down, and we don't blame the lady very much for refusing to give the celebrated architect his freedom for such a small amount.—Racine Journal-News.

Under some conditions it is a good investment to accept a proposition for a divorce without pecuniary stipulation. However, this seems to be a case where (W)right was wrong.

As a matter of fact, the prime object of any teacher is to carry his charge to the place where his guidance is unnecessary. The function of the preceptor is merely to indicate the right road. If the student himself refuses to traverse that road, the process is labor lost.—Wisconsin State Journal.

The prime object of any real teacher should be to explain the advantages and disadvantages of both roads and, at the same time, develop the mind of his charge until the latter is competent to make his own choice.

ALIEN PROPERTY SAFE.

Sheboygan Press—

February 28, 1919

The dispatch in the Press of Monday to the effect that at Racine a committee of three would be appointed to take charge of all alien property and make some disposition of it, using the proceeds for the purchase of Liberty Bonds, is somewhat misleading. This can only be done in cases where alien enemies have been found guilty of some crime against the government. For instance a man like Gessert and his sons might be penalized in this manner, but the government is very broad in matters of this kind. Enemy aliens have committed crimes against the United States which would have resulted in death in their native land, and it is to meet just such emergencies, that the government has issued an order to confiscate their property. Aliens from either Germany or Austria who have property, have no occasion for feeling alarmed about their property, so long as they live within the law. It is those that are plotting against this government, and going around and lying about Uncle Sam that have something to fear.

————O————

Dan. P. Boehm of the U. S. food administration announces that U. S. hens are going to lay 150 million more eggs than usual, between now and April 30. And, a year hence, every egg will fetch 6 cents, or thereabouts. Ain't hens the lovely financiers.

————O————

Some actor fellow has dramatized the book of Job and is going to produce it in New York. We predict its failure. Job had less patience than the average audience of today and won't interest anybody.

————O————

Pullman Company has decided to sell only one berth to one passenger hereafter. It'll go hard with a lot of fellows, being forced to sleep in one bed at a time.

————O————

Over 200,000,000 bushels of potatoes likely to go to waste. The heathen down in Peru would evaporate them and make them human food that would be good for months to come.

————O————

Ben Reitman announces his intention of dropping anarchism and devoting all his time to practicing medicine and writing poetry. We wish he'd reform altogether and practice medicine.

————O————

Japs may be fighting Germans, in Siberia, before long. It's about time for the Japanese to be fighting somebody, somewhere.

————O————

U. S. reactionaries must stand aside or get run over, says Professor Ross of Wisconsin University, who has just returned from Russia.

————O————

U. S. Indians have subscribed $9,000,000 to Liberty Loans and 5,000 of them have enlisted in army or navy. Lo! the rich and loyal indian!

————O————

Grand Duke Nicholas, whom the Bolsheviki are going to try to hang, was once "the hope of Russia." Maybe he is yet, and still will hang.

————O————

"The world is longing for peace," says Von Hertling. We violate no confidence in stating that it is also fighting for it.

Sheboygan Press-Telegram—
August 27, 1924

HOUSEHOLD SUGGESTIONS

Clean Out Closets

Go through your clothes closets, shelves and racks frequently and weed out the contents. Do not keep storing articles that have no value and which add to your work.

Frying Fish

Before putting fish into the frying pan put a small breadcrust into the grease. When it becomes a golden brown you will know the grease is at just the right temperature for the fish. Leave the crust in the pan and it will prevent the fat from sputtering.

Cut Large Pieces

Cook vegetables whole when practical, otherwise cut them into as large pieces as is convenient.

Fresh Vegetables

Wash all fresh vegetables no matter how clean they may look.

Old Brooms

When a broom has worn unevenly, soak it in hot suds, rinse and dry in the open air. Then cut the bristles evenly and you will find that you can still get much more service from it.

Cleaning Furniture

Clean gilt furniture or picture frames with a paste made of whiting and alcohol.

And That's That!

A Locally Conducted Column By W.J.P.

A Real Optimist

This is really a fact.

Five years ago a certain local gent built a garage and since that time has been attending all of the auto shows within range in order to win an automobile to put in his garage!

Suggestions Dept.

Indiana's champion onion-grower claims the onion is a member of the lily family.

Just the same we wouldn't advise any fellow to send his best girl a bouquet of onions.

[And any guy who does, doesn't know his onions.]

By Way Of Report

Excitement ran high on Sheboygan's northeast side the other night when a prominent citizen thought he spotted a "brown bear" in the streets. A call to the police department brought a squad car to the scene, and a policeman was all set to shoot when another officer discovered that the "bear" was just a huge dog.

[And that's not just a bear story, either.]

Observation

Dentists have been urged to use the word "remove" instead of "extract".

Just the same a tooth-pulling is a tooth-pulling, regardless of what you call it.

Just So You Know

There's one nice thing about it — there's no hazing in the electoral college.

Sheboygan Press—
November 18, 1936

Time Marches On

Air-cooled houses for pigs are suggested so that pigs can be raised all the year around.

At least the ventilation idea ought to be good.

News Comment

Item says stream-line education is being favored. [Especially co-eds?]

Add News Comments

"Music Aids Insane", says news headline.

But think of what the neighboring saxophonists, drummers and trombone players have done in an opposite direction!

Liars We All Know

"This is on the up-and-up."

Famous Last Words

"Excuse me."

W. J. P.

Backstairs In White House

United Press White House Writer

DENVER (UP) — Backstairs at the summer White House:

Mrs. John S. Doud, mother of the President's wife, likes dog racing. She frequently visits the local track when the fleet greyhounds thrill the pari-mutuel bettors on summer nights.

The President is no racing fan, however, and prefers to stay at Mrs. Doud's home evenings and chat or play bridge with old friends.

—— O ——

Before Mrs. Doud came west ahead of the President and Mrs. Eisenhower, her neighbors were alarmed one night to see flashlights playing ominously around the interior of the unoccupied house.

The neighbors spread the alarm, even called the newspapers. Breathless reporters and photographers who arrived minutes later discovered that the lights were being employed quite properly by Secret Service agents preparing for the President's visit.

—— O ——

The neighbors still can't get over seeing strange young men pacing in front of the Doud home as the Secret Service maintains a guard, as discreetly as possible, while the President is in residence there.

But old hands at this business predict the neighbors will become accustomed to the security precautions around the President and pay no more attention to it than did the neighbors of former President Truman in Independence, Mo.

—— O ——

Mr. Eisenhower moves about Denver—to his office at Lowry Air Force Base or to the golf course—with a minimum escort; no noisy motorbikes, but the Secret Service agents are always in their follow-up car.

—— O ——

Dick Flohr, who usually drives the President's air-conditioned limousine, is probably motordom's most active car polisher. Every time the President leaves the car, Flohr, a veteran Secret Service man, whips out a chamois and removes any fingerprints or dust which might mar the sheen of the nation's No. 1 car.

—— O ——

Tom Golden is a Denver detective who was loaned to Mr. Eisenhower as a security officer during the 1952 campaign. Golden, after the campaign, undoubtedly could have had a job with the new administration in Washington, but he preferred Denver.

When the President came out here last Saturday, as asked that Golden be assigned to the White House security force for the vacation—and for old time's sake. •

IT TOOK AN IRISHMAN, from Dacada yet, to come up with the winning name in the Jaycee B-Day pig-naming contest at Fountain Park, Saturday. Maurice Monahan, operator of a grocery store in that Ozaukee County village, sent in the winning entry to name the future Jaycee mascot. Her name "Cleobratra" of course. Donor of the frisky 40-pound porker was the Wisconsin Feeder Pig Co-operative, with headquarters at Francis Creek (Manito-woc County). With Monahan in Wood Veterans' Hospital, Mrs Monohan was on hand to receive the Jaycee first prize. She is shown here (right) with a firm hold on "Cleo" Others, from the left: Mrs James (Ellie) Paulmann, Jaycee contest chairman; Leslie Rahn, R. 2, Sheboygan, "Cleo's" caretaker for the day, and Mel Hoffmann, Jaycee B-Day general chairman — (Sheboygan Press photo).

Sheboygan Press—
October 13, 1917

Sheboygan Evening Press—
August 15, 1912

FOUND SKELETON ON ISLAND AT CRYSTAL LAKE

A skeleton buried six feet under ground was found by R. H. Willis of Glenbeulah this week on the island in Crystal Lake owned by Congressman Edward Voigt. On inspecting the cranium, it was found that a bullet had entered the temple, making a large hole in that spot. The bones were perfect, there was no sign of any box or casket, or any other materials, and the probability is that the person was shot many years ago, and buried on this lonely island.

The fact that the skeleton was found six feet under ground suggests a crime and not suicide, Mr. Willis said. It is not known, whether it is the skeleton of a white man or Indian.

FINDS OLD HORSESHOE.

Fifty years ago or longer, when Senator Isaac Stephenson was a young man and the primeval woods of Wisconsin had not yet made him a millionaire, a horse shoe, cast in a forest path, was hung over a branch of a young tree and forgotten. Recently a timber "cruiser" found the shoe deeply inbedded in the wood, and brought it to "Uncle Ike," who promptly gave him $10 for it. Senator Stephenson believes the shoe is of English iron, and it is evidently hand made.

"American iron was not good in those days," he said. "In the olden days, you know, there was a king whose horses had four golden shoes. One was lost, and the finder was supposed to reap good luck with the shoe. I suppose our fancy about good luck and horseshoes comes from that tale. Any way, the man who hung this shoe in the tree evidently remembered that proverb, and had a kind thought for whoever later found it."

The block of beechwood with its imbedded horseshoe lies on the senator's desk in his committee room.

Banked in Stove; Money Gone.

Cleveland, O.--James Carr, a mill worker, lost $1,419, part of the savings of his lifetime, when a fire was started in the kitchen stove, in which the money had been hidden. Now he is broke. The failure of a bank, in which part of his money had been placed, induced him to hide his savings in the stove. Mrs. Carr forgot and set fire to rubbish in it.

LOST IN AN ICE CAVE.

To be lost in an ice cave for 24 hours was the unpleasant experience of two Newark (N. J.) citizens recently. One of the victims, John Mohlenpah, says that he with six others, went to the cave, but with J S. Price, became separated from the others and lost his way. They burned part of their clothing to light the cavern, but when their last match was exhausted they found themselves in a four-foot cavern, with a bottomless pit on one side and a clig on the other. In a crouched position they remained there for 20 hours until rescuing parties found them. The men almost froze, but kept up circulation by constant rubbing. A party of 13 men, one of five rescuing parties, aided by 500 feet of rope, succeeded in dragging Mohlenpah and Price to safety,

and a crowd of anxious people greeted them at the entrance of the cavern. Mohlenpah had almost abandoned hope of escape.

STRANGE STORY OF A WATCH

A silver watch which he lost in a field 14 years ago has been recovered by Jacob L. Graybill near Manheim, Pa. The field was plowed and harrowed each year, and the watch was found recently by a workman. The crystal was unbroken, but the works were ruined.

Dog Bites Wooden Leg.

Asbury Park, N. J.—An ordinary family dog of regular habits was sleeping peacefully in the yard of Robert B. Culvert. The new baker ambled down from the house to the gate. As he swung it open there was a squeak that aroused the dog and the canine's teeth had pierced his pantaloons. The dog held fast to the leg

"Let go there, Flavors," commanded the dog's master. But the baker only smiled.

"Guess that dog will get foolish after awhile," he said quietly. "You know I have got a wooden leg." Culvert pried the dog loose.

Sheboygan Press—September 20, 1946

Hog Sets Record Price Of $8.80

Austin, Minn. — (UP) — A 245-pound Poland China barrow, exhibited by the Manning Creamery Co., Manning, Ia., set a new world price record when it brought $2,256 after being rated the individual champion of the National Barrow show.

The animal was purchased Thursday by Curly's cafe, Minneapolis, which paid $8.80 per pound for the pork. The previous record was $8.25 per pound.

Another world record was set at the same sale for a pen of three Chester Whites, shown by Portage farm, Woodville, O., which were sold to Swift & Co., Chicago, for $1,240, or $1.55 per pound for the 800-pound pen. The previous high was $1.30 per pound.

Other sales included a Berkshire boar, exhibited by Milo Wolrab, Mt. Vernon, Ia., for $1,025. The boar was purchased by Bern Grove farm, Palatinate, Ill. Approximately 2,000 hogs were sold at the auction held in conjunction with the swine show.

December 7, 1903

SWIMS INTO HARBOR

Escaped From Lincoln Park at Chicago about Three Weeks Ago.

"Big Ben" the sea lion that escaped from Lincoln park at Chicago about three weeks ago, appeared in this harbor yesterday and caused considerable excitement until he left, bound northward. The animal was first seen at the old Barry dock at the foot of Jefferson avenue, between eleven and twelve o'clock by Ed. Freyberg, who caught sight of the animal playing about the outlet of the sewer at that point Capt. Muntinga a well known fisherman soon appeared on the scene and also Capt. Dionne of the life saving station, who followed the animal about the river. It swam about until twelve thirty o'clock when it was seen to leave the mouth of the harbor by Capt. Dionne.

Later on in the afternoon many spectators saw the lion attempt to get on to the breakwater northeast of the harbor pier and then afterward he swam toward the shore and got out of the water on to the ice at the foot of Niagara avenue at the mouth of the sewer. When his pursuers approached, he slid back into the water and that was the last seen of him here.

A row boat was brought into use and young men armed with a gun patroled the ice bound beach as far north as the Point, without seeing him, they occasionaly firing off the gun with the idea of attracting the attention of the animal. Then two red lights were hung near the mouth of the Niagara avenue sewer as darkness drew near, but these did not attract the animal and the next time he will be heard from, will probably be from Manitwoc.

The animal has now visited Waukegan, Kenosha, Racine, Milwaukee and this port in regular order, swimming about the harbor and then leaving for the north. His antics could be plainly seen from the docks as he dove and rolled about in the river here yesterday.

There is a reward of $100 offered for the animal for his capture alive so that he may be returned to Lincoln park at Chicago.

If you were to drive from the Lincoln Park Zoo in Chicago to Blue Harbor Resort in Sheboygan you would travel approximately 144 miles.

Boy Bites Snake And That Is News!

When a snake bites a man—that's not news.

But when 17-months-old Jack Bone bit a snake, that was news.

Jack was playing in the yard. Not knowing better, he bit an 8-inch reptile—non-poisonous.

Jack's mother rushed him to the hospital for a treatment. He suffered no ill effects from the bite.

But the snake—poor snake—he died!

July 25, 1936

February 12, 1940

Frog Closes Water Main

Amherst, N. S. — (UP)— Post office employees went without water for nearly a day, and they couldn't figure out what was wrong. The building engineer finally performed an emergency plumbing operation and found a huge bullfrog was wedged into the main —dead.

Bratwurst Season Gets An Official Opening At Park

The Sheboygan Junior Chamber of Commerce officially opened the 1953 bratwurst season Thursday evening at a regular meeting at the Kiwanis Park Shelter House. Sixty -five members and guests took part in the program which included movies of the centennial "train robbery" and the March of Dimes street campaign.

Jaycees and their guests, including Mayor Edward C. Schmidt, Editor A. Matt. Werner of The Sheboygan Press, Association of Commerce President E. F. Klozotsky, Martin Rammer, Erwin L. Steiner, E. C. Hoyer, Merton Finger and Gene Hertel, discussed the possibility of a "National Bratwurst Day" in Sheboygan, the bratwurst center of the world.

President Len Wartman indicated that the promotional idea was received enthusiastically.

Clouds Of Smoke, Savory Aromas Prevail Here Today

Sheboygan Press — Thursday, August 13, 1953

It's Bratwurst Day in the "Wurst City of the World."

Events of the day-long celebration of Sheboygan's claim to fame as the Bratwurst Center of the World started at 8 a. m. when Larry S. MacDonald, chairman of the Junior Chamber of Commerce committee in charge of the festival, introduced A. Matt. Werner, editor and publisher of The Sheboygan Press, who officially opened the program with a brief address at the corner of Bratwurst Blvd. (N. 8th St.) and Wisconsin Ave.

Suggests Annual Observance

Mr. Werner, citing the growth of Sheboygan's reputation for the finest bratwurst in the world, pointed out that Bratwurst Day in Sheboygan can grow to rival the special days of other communities throughout the state and country. He suggested that the day be made an annual event to bring Sheboygan the fame it deserves as the "Wurst City" of the world, not the "wurst city" in the world.

He paid tribute to Sheboygan Jaycees who are manning fryers and stands at every downtown intersection and urged community-wide support of the festival which makes its debut as a highlight of the city's centennial celebration.

A long line of customers greeted the Jaycees who started serving "brats" at the Wisconsin Ave. stand at 8 a. m. and by mid morning the familiar clouds of smoke and savory aromas were rising at stands at every downtown intersection

Extensive Entertainment

Bratwurst lunch began at 11 a. m. and 1 p. m. entertainment began in the downtown area. At 2 o'clock the contest to name one of eight contestants as Sheboygan bratwurst queen began at Fountain Park. The queen will be crowned by Charles Coburn, the movie and television star, who is taking part in the centennial celebration here.

The contestants, each backed by a local store, included: Pat Kroos, Corliss Lannoye, Royola Lienau, Loretta Luedke, Delores Stoelb, Wilma Teller, Audrey Theobald and Beverly Wodach.

A contest to determine Sheboygan bratwurst eating champion opened at 3:30 p. m. at Fountain Park and was followed by a square dancing exhibition by the Turner Square Dancing Club at 4:30 p. m. at the corner of Bratwurst Blvd. and Wisconsin Ave.

Entertainment in the downtown area will continue this evening with the Original Oomph Band, the Sheboygan Barbershop Chorus and quartets, the Balkan Serenaders and the Polka Rascals taking part in the program.

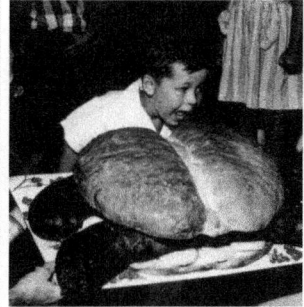

Sheboygan Press — July 31, 1954

Who Will Be The Bratwurst King Of Sheboygan For '54?

Who will be the bratwurst eating king of Sheboygan for 1954?

The honor, gained during last summer's original Bratwurst Day by Roger Theobald, will be conferred upon the winner of this year's competition — to be held at 3:30 p.m. next Saturday, Aug. 7, in Fountain Park.

In winning the 1953 title Champ Theobald consumed the grand total of nine single "brats." The runnerup did away with eight.

This year, however, the contestants will be called upon to tangle with double "brats."

Theobald has already indicated that he is in training for a determined bid to defend the crown he won last year at centennial time.

Anyone interested in competing next Saturday will be required to fill out the accompanying entry blank and mail it to Robert Richter at The Sheboygan Press. Deadline for entries will be next Friday, Aug. 6.

BRATWURST DAY
— Eating Contest —

Saturday, August 7 at 3:30 p. m.
FOUNTAIN PARK

Name ....

Address ....

Age .... Phone ....

Entries to be submitted no later than Friday, Aug. 6 to:
Robert Richter, The Sheboygan Press, Sheboygan, Wis.

Sheboygan Press — August 14, 1924

Ostrich Race

Both ostriches were like bucking broncos. It took two or three men to hold them when they were ready to go, and after they started they cut up a number of performances before completing the circuit around the race track. The most manageable one did quite well traveling without hesitancy almost around the track, until it arrived at the west side, where it reached a point that was thickly populated with spectators. Then it gave a demonstration of how stubborn a feathered creature of that tpye can be.

The youngster that tried to ride the other is in all probability nursing some sore spots on his body as the result of being thrown from the bird's back a number of times. The ostrich apparently did not like its burden, and would not go far at a time before it would stop and dump the boy. Then it necessitated a long chase to catch him and start over.

Once while he was being chased, he walked up to the edge of the race track at the south end of the Fair grounds and looked over the low fence. In his quest for the possibilities of getting over it he leaned against it somewhat heavily and overbalanceed, falling over it on his back. It took some of the spectators besides the handlers to capture the bird and lift him over the fence.

Feed Them Oranges

Before the birds were started on their jaunts around the track, they were each given a number of helpings to oranges. Feeding them proved highly entertaining to the spectators, especially the children. It was possible to watch the course of the fruit down the elongated neck of the bird. Its progress was seen by the round bulging appearance of the neck as it proceeded to travel downward.

For the first time in the history of the fair silver foxes are being exhibited by the Sheboygan Fox & Fur Co.

The O'Connor Sisters sang a number of popular songs by band accompaniment, and their selections were well given.

The Ueno Japs in their tumbling and other gymnastic and foot juggling work put on one of the best acts that has ever been given on a fair program here.

The Geddis Trio combined neatness and originality in their thrilling exhibition of aerial and bar stunts.

One of the most laugh provoking numbers seen around here was the Marco twins, one tall and a contortionist of no slight ability, and the other short and rotund.

Madame Bedine and Victor Bedine gave a splendid exhibition with their trained horses large and small, their dogs and monkeys.

The Royal American Shows a carnival company furnished many interesting attractions on the midway during the afternoon and evening.

Are these your relatives?

None of us have been lucky enough to claim them...

The two cylinder, four passenger "Brotz Special" made by Mr. Brotz in 1902-1904 from his own designs. Motor and parts were turned out on a foot power lathe. All parts —chassis, post steering apparatus, transmission, rear axle—were made at home. Mr. Brotz is at the wheel with Mrs. Brotz. The Brotz children occupy the front "rumble seat."

AUTO DROPS TEN FEET, TURNS TURTLE, PINS EIGHT DOWN NO ONE SERIOUSLY HURT

No this is not a Ford story, but it is a real one just the same.

Saturday afternoon George Klahn, of Greenbush, purchased a Studebaker car and immediately took his first lesson in driving the car. He handled it so well that on Sunday afternoon he took his wife and family and hired man and wife for a spin.

There were eight in the car and all enjoyed the ride immensely. Reaching home late in the afternoon Mr Klahn started to drive the car into the barn when, it is presumed he became confused and instead of applying the brakes, threw on more power The car shot through the barn, crashed through the wall, fell ten feet, turned turtle and pinned the eight passengers under the car.

They managed to crawl out and upon investigation found Mr. Klahn was the only one injured and he received one broken rib. The car war badly damaged

AUTO GOES OVER AN EMBANKMENT

At the conclusion of the Business Men's banquet last night, a traveling man who makes this town regularly, borrowed T. M. Bowler's automobile to take a friend home. The two headed west on Center avenue at a fairly good pace. The avenue ends abruptly on the west side of N. Water street, adjoining the Rochlus flour and feed store. The stranger was evidently not aware of this fact and drove the car straight on. The night was pitch dark and the stranger did not realize the danger ahead until within a few feet of the embankment. The brakes were hastily set and both occupants leaped from the car just as it went over the bank. It was a miraculous escape. The car plunged nearly to the hubs in the sand below and was removed this morning. No damage was done but the driver and his friend will probably always remember it as a most fortunate escape.

DANGEROUS SPOT.

This particular spot is a most dangerous one at all times and several citizens who witnessed the raising of the automobile this morning, remarked that the city ought to put up some kind of a guard there immediately.

FENDER SAVES LIFE OF CHILD

Youngster Run Down at Michigan avenue and Eleventh street is Scooped up like a Potato on a Shovel---Runs Away Unhurt.

A little girl had a narrow escape today at Michigan avenue and Eleventh street when she was struck by a street car and scooped up on the fender, without injuries, apparently, for the moment the car came to a stop the youngster ran away. The car crew endeavored to find out her name and address, but the youngster fled so quickly that this was not accomplished.

It appears that the child had became confused when she saw the car bearing down upon her, and had run in front of it. The fender, which has proved the means of saving many lives since its humane introduction into car traffic years ago, did its work promptly, and the kidlet was scooped up like a potato on a shovel. She screamed just once, and then, when the car stopped, laughed and ran away. The child was about 9 years old, bystanders said.

Charleston Daily Mail - Charleston, West Virginia, - June 11, 1922

Wisconsin Survivor of Maine Tells His Story

Sheboygan, Wis., June 10 - When most Wisconsin survivors of famous events want to talk over experiences which they have undergone, they can call some of their fellow survivors together; but there is one man here who must do his "discussing" alone.

George Fox, so far as known, is the only man in Wisconsin who can claim the honor of being a survivor of the blowing up of the Maine, the tragedy which sent this nation to war with Spain.

Fox says he owes his life to a spasm of economy in the navy at the time of the explosion. One of the regulations at the time was that in order to save coal, all dynamos should be turned off at midnight. It was Fox's job to keep the oil lamps burning after that time.

The night of the explosion, Fox said, he had just completed his tour of inspection and had laid down to snatch a few moments rest. He had scarcely fallen asleep, he says, when he awoke to find himself lying on top of a huge mass of hot and twisted steel. He hastily dove overboard and was soon picked up by one of the small Spanish boats coming to the aid of the Maine. He said he was taken to a Spanish hospital and well treated.

Immortality Achieved by Three Victims of Streetcar Crash

It was exactly 8:44am on Thursday February 9, 1911. Along the Sheboygan's main business district, North Eighth Street, shades were being raised, stores were opening, salesmen were adding up change in their cash registers and looking forward to another day's work. The Lake View street car of the Sheboygan Railway and Electric Company was picking up passengers in front of the Foeste Hotel.

It was a day like any other. But, within the next six minutes, the time it took the street car to ramble down the hill, into the dip and up to the Eight Street bridge one of the most bizarre accidents in Sheboygan County history would occur. Three people would lose their lives.

Tragedy Relived for Months
And the aftermath of those three minutes would not even begin to died down for at least two months. According to testimony that would be given later, George Thieme, the motorman of the Lake View car, had arrived in Sheboygan from Plymouth shortly before beginning the run. He had stopped at a local tavern and drunk one glass of beer — only one. It was something that he frequently did. He enjoyed a beer after breakfast.

Thieme was already under something of a cloud. Only the winter before a street car which he had been driving had run over and killed a little girl in front of Prange's department store. He had been absolved of all blame in the accident, but the association was still there.

Ernest Gonzenbach, general manager of the street car company, later said, almost defensively, that Thieme "is one of the best men I've got." He was next in line for a promotion. Gonzenbach said to the electric interurban line.

That morning he took on his passengers in front of the Foeste Hotel and continued on down North Eighth Street.

At the street car company's office he stopped and picked up a new conductor, a man known only as Weber. One other passenger got on.

And the streetcar continued on down North Eighth Street, picking up speed. The rails, Thieme later said, were slippery and probably coated with ice.

The streetcar was traveling at about 20 miles per hour when it hit the bottom of the dip below the hill.

Drawbridge Opening

Suddenly, according to Thieme, he looked up and noticed that the bridge tender of the Eighth Street bridge was stretching chains across the street to block the traffic over the river. The drawbridge was opening to allow the tugboat Peter Reiss to pass through.

George Thieme, for a fleeting instant, wondered whether he could stop in time.

From that moment on, everything was confusion.

Thieme later stated that he applied the brakes immediately, and when he found that they were having absolutely no effect, he put the streetcar in reverse gear to bring the car to a halt. He also pulled the lever dumping sand from a box beneath the car onto the tracks.

But, the streetcar continued unhesitatingly on. An electrical circuit breaker located 81 feet north of the bridge had released when the drawbridge began to pull to one side, cutting off all power to the car. The reverse gear simply didn't take, and the tracks were too slippery for the brakes to hold.

The streetcar rolled slowly on, like a ship riding the crest of a soft wave. Finally, Thieme shouted, " I can't hold her!" and for the first time for passengers and Conductor Weber realized something was wrong.

Women, Girl Trapped

Immediately two men standing on the rear platform, Joseph Mosich of 1529 Union Avenue, and a street car company employee named Sam Dodgson, leaped from the moving car.

A third man, a "traveling man" from Milwaukee named P.W. Etzold who had been sitting in the car jumped to his feet, snagged his rubber on something, fell flat on his face in the middle of the aisle, scrambled to his feet again and took a running jump from the rear of the car.

Two women and a girl who had been sitting in the car didn't move. Then the car plunged.

In the words of the Sheboygan Press: "As the car went off the rails, the wheels striking the stone abutments, the cars seemed to rise in the air for just a second, and then took its fatal plunge. The iron chain which was strung the full width of the opening snapped like a cord as the car struck it and flying links went in all directions."

The car turned over completely once, then struck and righted itself before it sank in nine feet of water.

Motorman, Conductor Saved

Left dangling in astonished silence from a cross-brace of the bridge was Conductor Weber, who had leaped just as the car began to go down. Someone, charitably, pulled him back onto the bridge.

George Thieme, a trifle slower, had dropped into the icy water. He clung for a few seconds to a floating cake of ice and finally found one of the loose ends of the chain.

The two women, Miss Anna Mather, 53, a Sheboygan Falls music teacher; and Miss Tannie Alice Van Ouwerkerk, 20, a teacher in Sheboygan's Second Ward School, were still trapped in the car. So was the girl, 14-year old Olga Willimite of 2006 Superior Avenue.

They drowned before workmen aboard the tugboat Peter Reiss could chop holes in the roof of the car to get them out.

An inquest was called immediately by Coroner Peter Feagan, and indignant citizens jammed the courtroom by the hundreds to witness it. For five straight days The Press headlined the story, devoting almost the entire front page to it. Throughout the entire town, people were talking of little else.

The bridge tender and the captain of the tug boat, as well as a dozen or more witnesses, all testified at the inquest that the drawbridge had been at least two-thirds open by the time the street car had approached it. George Thieme denied this time and again.

Manslaughter Charge Filed

The six-man coroner's jury apparently refused to believe him, however. After deliberating for over five and a half hours they ruled that Thieme had been guilty of negligence. He had been going too fast, they said, and failed to observe the open bridge.

The Sheboygan Press headlined the story in an extra edition that hit the streets at 9:15p.m., 35 minutes after the verdict was in.

And the following day Thieme was arrested and charged with manslaughter in the fourth degree.

After these fast-moving first days, the finale to the incident had to wait for almost two months, however, and it was decidedly anti-climactic. Thieme's case came up before the April session of Circuit Court, the whole incident was examined a second time, and after two and a half hours of deliberation **the jury decided he was innocent.**

On April 19, 1911, Thieme finally found himself a free man.

But the tragic incident simply refused to die. For years the newspapers commemorated it, the people talked about it, strangers were taken to view the scene.

N. 8th St. Bridge, where street car plunged in the river and 8 lives were lost, Feb. 9, '11.   SHEBOYGAN, WIS.

Above: Looking south on Eighth Street in Sheboygan.

Below: Interurban car being removed from the Sheboygan River after plunging off the 8th Street Bridge.

N. 8th St. Bridge, where street car plunged in the river and 8 lives were lost, Feb. 9, '11.   SHEBOYGAN, WIS.

N. 8th St. Bridge, where street car plunged in the river and 5 lives were lost, Feb. 9, '11. SHEBOYGAN, WIS.

ACCIDENT FATAL TO SHEBOYGAN BOY

Bicycle Rider And Interurban Have Collision

April 20, 1928

Returning from a bicycle ride to Black River at about 6:30 p. m. Thursday, William Schmezer, 14, son of Mr. and Mrs. Carl Schmezer, 1102 Union avenue, collided with a Milwaukee Northern passenger car at Stop 49 and suffered injuries from which he died in St. Nicholas hospital this morning.

Injuries which resulted in death this morning included a crushed head, double fracture of a leg, fracture of the collar bone, lacerations of the head, legs and thighs, and internal injuries.

The youth, accompanied by Willis Jensen, 13, son of Mr. and Mrs. John Beekman, 2416 S. Seventh street, had gone for a ride in the country so they could enjoy themselves without being constantly in fear of automobile traffic, and they were returning home when the tragic collision occurred at the intersection of the Northern tracks and S. Twelfth street, known as Stop No. 49.

Neither of the boys went home after school, according to a statement made by Willis Jensen this morning. As soon as they left school they took their bicycles and rode out to Black river on S. Ninth street. After spending some time out there they started back home by way of Twelfth street.

Companion's Explanation

"William was quite a ways ahead of me," said Willis. "He did not see the interurban coming, but I did, and I hollered to him to stop. I guess he didn't hear me in time, for he ran into the front step of the car, which was coming from the south, and was thrown into the ditch."

Floyd Grayson, 1011 N. Eleventh street, motorman on the car, and Garret Huibregtse, Jefferson avenue, conductor, picked the injured boy up after the interurban was stopped and brought him and the Jensen youth to Sheboygan. The city ambulance here called at the Milwaukee Northern station and conveyed the accident victim to the hospital, where every attention possible was given by physicians.

Mr. and Mrs. Schmezer were called to the hospital, and they were beside their son continuously up to the time of his death, which occurred at about 5:30 a. m. today.

Mrs. Schmezer said this morning that she was alarmed as to the whereabouts of William, and had called several places in efforts to find him. A premonition that something had happened prompted her to call the police station and the clinic to ascertain whether he had figured in an accident, fearing the possibility that he had collided with an automobile while on his way home from school.

Agent's Statement

W. Carlson, local agent for the Milwaukee Northern, gave out the following statement about the accident in behalf of Andrew Kordick, superintendent of the company, at Cedarburg:

"The boys were playing along the road. One was ahead of the other and was looking back to the one behind him. Some farmers who were nearby saw the approaching interurban and shouted to the boys, but they apparently did not hear, and the Schmezer boy's bicycle ran into the front step of the car, throwing him into the ditch. Both of the boys were put on the car and brought to Sheboygan. The Schmezer boy was immediately removed to the clinic after the car got in."

Motorman Grayson was on duty today and could not be reached, but Mr. Carlson said that the foregoing statement is in substance the report that Mr. Grayson made to the office at Cedarburg.

The train figuring in the accident is known as Passenger No. 40, and is due in Sheboygan from Milwaukee at 6:36 p. m.

William Schmezer was born in Germany May 29, 1914, and came to this country with his parents in 1924. They lived in Calumet, Mich., two years before coming here. He and Willis Jensen were pupils of the Seventh grade, Longfellow school, and he attended Sunday school at St. Andrew's Lutheran church. He is the only child of Mr. and Mrs. Carl Schmezer.

Funeral services will be held Monday, the Rev. Mr. Beyer of St. Andrew's church officiating. Services will be at the home at 1:30 p. m. and at St. Andrew's church at 2 p. m. The body was removed to A. W. Ramm's undertaking parlors this morning.

Christmas Joys!
ELECTRICAL APPLIANCES!

Here are gifts that are certain to make her Christmas one of joy. Picture her delight—on Christmas morning—when she steps into the parlor and finds there on the table—an Electric Iron—an Electric Percolator—an Electric Chafing Dish — a Vacuum Cleaner — and many articles from our store that will aid her in the home.

SPECIALS

Flapper Electric Curling Irons at 99c

Electric Percolators, priced at $5.00 up to $13.00

Electric Toasters, special at $5.98

Electric Flat Irons, fully guaranteed, special at $3.98

Prange-Geussenhainer Co.

THE WINCHESTER STORE

802-804 North Eighth St.   Phone 302

Sheboygan Press—
December 20, 1923

Sheboygan Press—November 26, 1938

Dear Santa Claus:
I am a boy of ten years of age. Please bring me a pencil box with three pencils and a eversharp pencil, a fountain pen and two neckties and a writing desk.
From your friend,
Hyacinth Casper.

Dear Santa Claus:
I am a little girl 6 years old and am going to tell you what I want for Xmas. I want a pair of shoes and a pair of socks and a sled and a table and chairs and dishes and bring me some candy and nuts.
Goodby.
Mildred Warner, Plymouth.

Dear Santa Claus:
Will you please bring me a doll a doll buggy and Christmas tree candy and nuts. I am a girl six years old I was a good girl.
Yours truly,
Ruth Warner, Plymouth.

Dear Santa Claus:
I am a little girl 8 years old and am going to tell you what I want for Xmas. I would like a game of old maid and a writting desk and a nice pair of socks and dont forget my sisters and brothers and bring me some candy and nuts please.
Good by.
Lucia Warner, Plymouth.

Dear Santa Claus:
I am five years old and go to school every day. Please bring me a train with tracks, jumping jack, drum, new suit and a pair of new shoes. Please don't forget candy and nuts and a nice Christmas tree, with electric lights, and don't forget the starving children in Germany.
Your little boy,
Wm. Miller Jr.

Dear Santa:
Please bring me a wagon, a tree, a horse, and please dont forget the harness. Bring some nuts and candy and don't forget my Mamma and Daddy. I am now three years old and was a good boy all the time.
A Good boy,
Ralph Dippel, Cascade.

Dear Santa Claus:
I would like to have you bring me a steam engine, some skies, two books, electric train, and a lot of candy, some games, a gold belt buckle, and don't forget my mamma and papa and sister and grandmother and grandfather and all the poor children and not my christmas tree.
Good by.
Robert Hartenberger.

Dear Santa Claus:
I would like to have a bat and ball and a football and a flashlight and a bike and a pair of ice skates and a game and a laigtrig train and a drum and a horn.
Gottlieb Henning.

Santa Forced To Thumb Ride During Parade

Steubenville, Ohio.—(P)—Steubenville children hope Santa Claus doesn't have as much trouble getting around December 25 as he had here November 25.

Starting a Christmas parade with his reindeer and sleigh, Santa soon had to get out and hold up the deer, which couldn't keep their footing on the icy street.

Then the reindeer fell and one broke a leg.

The parade passed on, leaving Santa stranded.

He tried to catch up by running, but he was too fat. Out of breath, he "thumbed" the first vehicle that came along.

Throughout the rest of the parade Santa perched cheerfully on the running board of a national guard ambulance.

Health Hints

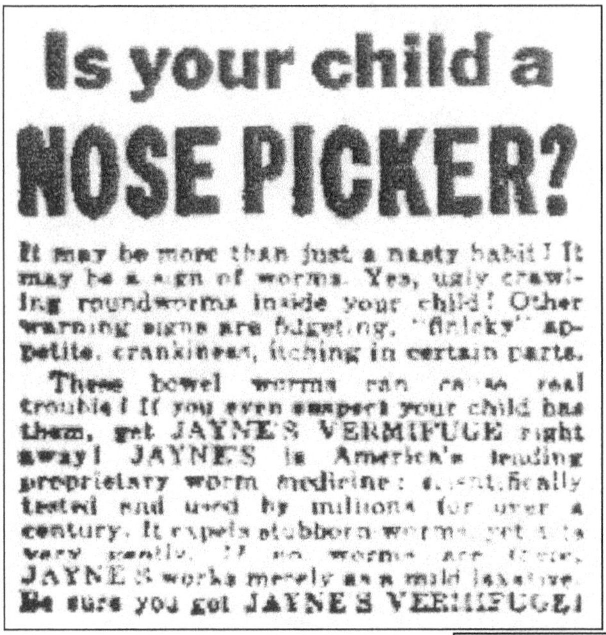

Is your child a NOSE PICKER?

It may be more than just a nasty habit! It may be a sign of worms. Yes, ugly crawling roundworms inside your child! Other warning signs are fidgeting, "finicky" appetite, crankiness, itching in certain parts.

These bowel worms can cause real trouble! If you even suspect your child has them, get JAYNE'S VERMIFUGE right away! JAYNE'S is America's leading proprietary worm medicine: scientifically tested and used by millions for over a century. It expels stubborn worms, yet it is very gently. If no worms are there, JAYNE'S works merely as a mild laxative. Be sure you get JAYNE'S VERMIFUGE!

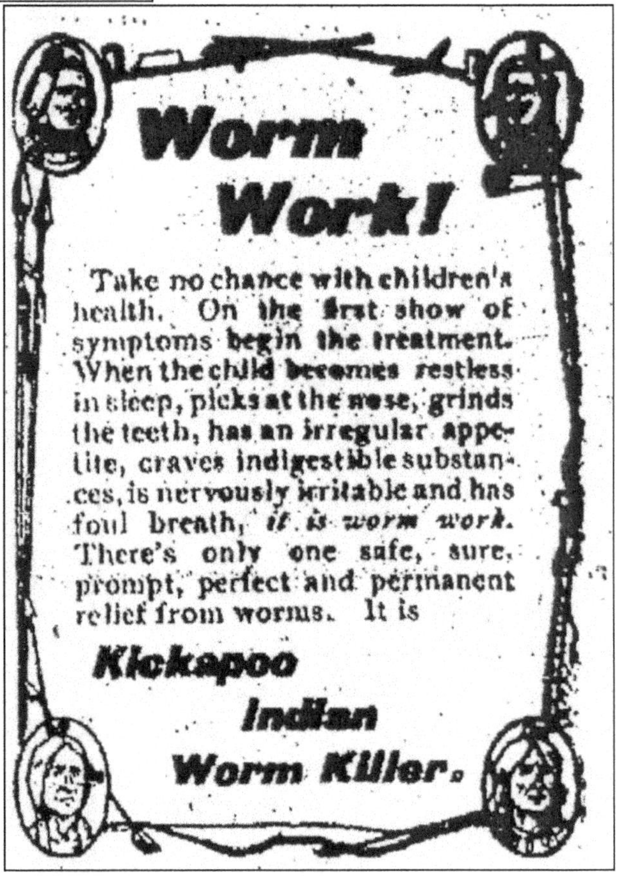

Worm Work!

Take no chance with children's health. On the first show of symptoms begin the treatment. When the child becomes restless in sleep, picks at the nose, grinds the teeth, has an irregular appetite, craves indigestible substances, is nervously irritable and has foul breath, *it is worm work*. There's only one safe, sure, prompt, perfect and permanent relief from worms. It is

Kickapoo

Indian

Worm Killer.

SHEB Herald   OCT 11/1890

A man who wanted to learn what profession he would have his son enter put him in a room with a Bible an apple and a dollar bill. If he found him reading the Bible when he returned he would make a clergyman of him; if he was eating the apple he should be a farmer; if he was interested in the dollar bill, a banker. He returned to find the boy sitting on the Bible with the dollar bill in his pocket and the apple almost devoured. He made a politician of him.

Many School Children are Sickly

Mothers who value their own comfort and the welfare of their children, should never be without a box of Mother Gray's Sweet Powders for Children, for use throughout the season. They Break up Colds. Relieve Feverishness, Constipation, Teething, Disorders, Headache and Stomach Troubles. Used by mothers for over 30 years. THESE POWDERS GIVE SATISFACTION. All Drug Stores. Don't accept any substitute.

Blackberry Cordial.

This is an excellent remedy for summer illness in teething children. Is also good as a summer drink. Warm and squeeze blackberries. To each pint of the juice add one pound of sugar, one and one-half teaspoonfuls of ground cinnamon, three-fourths tablespoonful mace, two teaspoonfuls cloves, boil all together for a quarter of an hour, strain, and to each pint add a glass of French brandy. If the attack is violent give a tablespoonful four or five times a day; less for children.

Sheboygan Press— September 28, 1911

WRITE YOUR NAME ON A BOMB FOR JAPAN
Bombs On Display At Prange's

Sheboygan Press— April 28, 1943

For the next three days a concerted effort will be made to sell more bonds at the booth in the H. C. Prange Store, and every purchaser will have an opportunity to write his or her name on a 500-pound bomb aimed for Japan.

Prange's War Bond booth, which has been the channel for the purchase of a good many bonds since the start of the war, now is the scene of Sheboygan's first actual contact with bombs which its dollars are purchasing. Along the rear outer wall of the booth stand three tremendous "500" bombs, almost five feet tall, resting on fins similar to the ones manufactured by our own Garton Toy company. These ugly, blunt-nosed weapons of war are frequently used in "skip -bombing", where a plane approaches the side of a ship at three or four hundred miles per hour at an elevation of about 50 feet. The technique gets its name from the skipping action of the bomb when it skitters across the surface of the water. Timing on the part of the pilot is vital in the above operation as the bombs are released close to the target.

When used for land bombing the approximate effective fragmentation area is 1,200 yards. The weight of the bomb casing is 250 pounds and its loaded weight is 500 pounds, from which derives the name "500" commonly used in referring to this type. The load material is TNT and the cost of each individual bomb is $200.

Extending on either side and behind the bombs are placards which bear the wording: "Let's help bomb Japan! For the next three days you have a chance to buy bonds here to send these bombs to Tojo. When you buy a bond write your name on one of these bombs. The more we write the mere avenging material for Pearl Harbor. Make this booth the most popular place in Sheboygan. Put your name on a bomb for Hirohito."

The first to purchase a bond from Miss Beverly Jane MacBride, who is in charge of the booth, was Mrs. Ferdinand W. DeSombre of 2224 N. Tenth street who signed one of the bombs before leaving.

These bombs will be carefully crated when they leave Sheboygan so that the signatures on them will not be mutilated in any way, and will actually be used by our boys in bombing the enemy. The bombs were consigned to the state chair-

H. C. PRANGE CO.

Buy A Bond!....
Sign your name on a BOMB for Hirohito

Bombs on Display at our
VICTORY BOOTH
STREET FLOOR

The Suits—
19⁹⁵ to 39⁹⁵

The Coats—
$22⁹⁵

Conscientious Suits ...

The suits are simple . . . but never stark . . . they're decorated with bows or braid . . . and the new shorter jackets and narrower skirts are neater and more attractive, besides being more careful of cloth. . In crepes, shetlands, twills, tropical worsteds and men's wear flannels.

Obliging Coats ...

The Sportleigh coats are clean cut and purposeful . . . styled for victory versatility. Classics they are and you can wear them smartly for sports occasions, daytime and even informal evening wear. And because they're so practical, you can wear them season after season.

Standbys of your wardrobe this season and for many to come, these conscientious suits and obliging coats are what the fashion-wise call "good buys".. You'll find them right here at Prange's . . . coats and suits with a crowded, useful career.

Sportleigh

Fashion Shop — Second Floor

They give their lives . . . you lend your money.

Buy More Bonds ... Victory Booth, Street Floor.

man and are more timely for the closing days of the $13,000,000,000 bond drive.

At left: H.C. Prange advertisement for women's suits crowing, Buy a Bond! Sign Your Name on a Bomb for Hirohito.

The bombs were on display at the Victory Booth on the Street Floor.

There were also conscientious suits, simple, but classic and Obliging Coats, clean cut and purposeful.

They Gave Their Lives . . . You Lend Your Money.

Buy More Bonds, Victory Booth, Street Floor

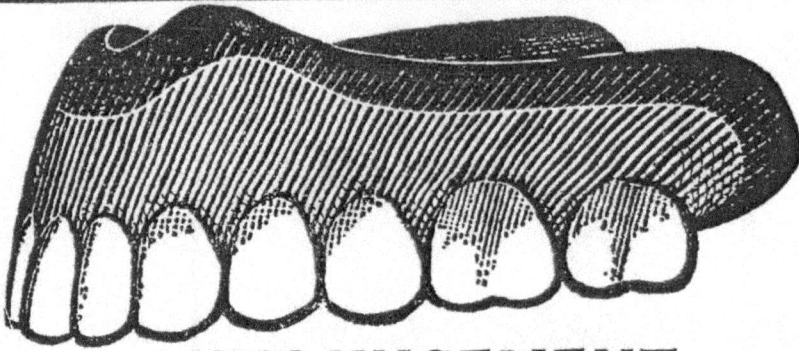

ANNOUNCEMENT

We wish to announce the opening of our new Dental Offices, where it is now possible for the people of Sheboygan to secure

Reliable Dentistry at Reasonable Rates

In order to introduce our new system of Painless Dentistry, Latest Methods and Reliable Workmanship, we will make the following prices

Until June 1st, 1929

After That Date We Will Raise Our Prices

GOOD SET OF TEETH (each)	$15.00	GOLD FILLINGS	$2.00 up
LIFE LIKE PLATES for	$20.00	PORCELAIN FILLINGS	$2.00 up
BRIDGE WORK or TEETH WITHOUT PLATES	$5.00 to $7.00	PORCELAIN CROWNS	$6.00
GOLD CROWNS (22 karat fine)	$5.00 to $7.00	SILVER FILLINGS	75c up
GOLD INLAYS	$2.00 up	PAINLESS EXTRACTION	75c

Allowance made on extracting when replaced by Plates or Bridge Work. Only the BEST materials used. Work guaranteed 10 years.

This is a conservative community, with sane, sensible people — people who appreciate real values and fair dealings. This may possibly be our first introduction to you, so we say it boldly, that we are of the NEW ERA in DENTISTRY; we believe in Honest Advertising, Honest Work, and Honest Prices. Our equipment and skill enables the production of the highest class dental work obtainable, and that, too, at a moderate fee, a price you can afford to pay.

WE WILL FORFEIT $1000

if work is not done in our offices in a first class manner, using the best materials. Examination free.

HARVEY (SYSTEM) DENTISTS

TERMINAL BLDG.

Entrance 809 Pennsylvania Ave.
S. W. Cor. N. 8th Street & Pennsylvania Ave.

Over Terminal Drug Store
Phone 4082

Offices at Chicago, Waukegan, Kankakee, Sterling, Galesburg, LaSalle, Freeport, Moline, Illinois, Davenport, Iowa and Watertown, Kenosha, and Racine Wis

Open Daily 9 A. M. to 8 P. M.
Closed Saturday Night at 5 P. M. No Sunday Hours

Dr. Geo. E. Krueger   Dr. M. R. Harvey   Dr. E. G. Clarke

1882.

SPRING OPENING

CLOTHING.
—AND—

Latest Styles

—OF—

SUITINGS

—FOR THE—

SPRING TRADE

A Full Line of Spring Goods for all kinds of Garments; also a Large Stock of Felt and soft Hats and Caps, Rubber Coat and Leggings, and Gents' Furnishing Goods in Shirts, Collars, Cuffs Etc., Etc., are now open for inspection at

JOHN NEVER'S,

Sheboygan Falls & Waldo.

BRYANT KERR, D.D.S.

GRADUATE OF THE

Pennsylvania College
of Dental Surgery.

Successor to

DR. L. A. POWELL.

DENTAL ROOMS - - BADES BLOCK.
PLYMOUTH WIS.

Operations in all Branches of Dentistry at reasonable prices. Nitrous Oxide Gas used for the Painless Extraction of teeth. Seven years of practical experience.

THE SUPERIOR BRANDS OF

PATENT FLOUR,

WINTER

And Spring Wheat
and Rye Flour,

— Manufactured by —

BRICKBAUER & KLUMB,

— of the —

South Plymouth Mills,

are unexcelled,

And with the other Mill Merchandise are delivered free of charge in any part of the city.

Merchant and Custom Grinding.

☞ CASH PAID FOR WHEAT. ☜

ALFONSO.

The thoroughbred Spanish Jack, 3 years old, will be put to a limited number of mares this season.

Those wishing to put mares to him apply at Glenbeulah.

JAMES SHUFFLEBOTHAM.

FINE CARRIAGES.

Thurman & Kœllmer's

SPRING SALE OF

Carriages,
Platform Wagons
and Buggies

Have been Unprecedentedly Large.

STOCK the LARGEST

—AND—

Prices the Cheapest

IN THE CITY.

Just Received Full Lines of

TOP AND OPEN BUGGIES,
PHÆTONS, TIMPKIN SPRINGS,
AND FINE CARRIAGES.

Also a Large Amount of Work of their Own Manufacture.

THURMAN & KŒLMER.

Plymouth, Wis.

G. T. Loomis, M. D.,

Physician and Surgeon,

Cascade, Wis.

Office hours from 10 to 12 A. M. and from 6 to 6 P. M.

J. F. Hauenstein,

Hardware!

Stoves, Tinware, Etc.,

SHEBOYGAN FALLS. WIS.

Drs. PRICE & BREWER

HAVE VISITED

OSHKOSH

TWENTY YEARS.

Have met with unparalleled success in the treatment of all

Chronic Diseases

—OF THE—

THROAT, HEART, LUNGS,
STOMACH, LIVER.

Head, nerves, kidneys, bladder, womb and blood affections of the urinary organs, gravel, scrofula, rheumatism, catarrh, asthma, bronchitis, dyspepsia, &c. Drs. Price & Brewer's reputation has been acquired by candid, honest dealing and years of successful practice.

Our practice, not on experiment, but founded on the laws of Nature, with years of experience and evidence to sustain it, does not 'tear down, make sick to make well; no harsh treatment, no trifling, no flattering. We know the cause and the remedy needed; no guess work, but knowledge gained by years of experience in the treatment of chronic diseases exclusively; no encouragement without a prospect. Candid in our opinions, reasonable in our charges, claim not to know everything or cure everybody, but do lay claim to reason and common sense. We invite the sick, no matter what their ailment, to call and investigate before they abandon hope, make interrogations and decide for themselves. It will cost nothing as consultation is free. Visits made regularly.

Residence and Laboratory, Evanston, Ill.

Drs. Price & Brewer can be consulted at

Quitquioc House, Plymouth, Wis.

FRIDAY, Aug. 1, 1882.

—A—

COMPLETE STOCK

—OF—

Pure Drugs & Medicines

— Is Kept Constantly on Hand at —

W. J. BRIER'S

DRUG STORE

— Where can be found also a fine selection of —

TOILET ARTICLES,
PERFUMES, STATIONERY,

Musical Instruments

&c., &c., &c.

Prescriptions Carefully Compounded at all hours.

BAY and LAKE TRIPS

THROUGH THE BEAUTIFUL

GREEN BAY COUNTRY

TO

Petoskey and Mackinac Island

Leaving Green Bay Every Thursday at 9:30 P. M.

5 DAYS TRIP $16.00

Including Meals and Berth

Send for Folder with full Information

Green Bay Transportation Co.

Green Bay, Wis.

Sheboygan Press — June 20, 1912

THE CONVERTIBLE CAR $1,000.00

24 H. P., Touring Car, Roadster, Delivery Car (Three in One.)

$1,250   30 H. P., Fully Equipped $1,250

Drivers Seat on Left Side. The Coming Correct Position.

$500   RUNABOUT, 12 H. P., 1 CYLINDER $500

The only Electric Charging Plant in the City. Open Day and Night. Under charge of Competent Operators.

The Wilke Garage

Located in Business Center of City. Handy to all Principal Business Houses and Hotels.

Phones: Garage White 493
Residence White 1032. **706 Center Avenue.**

Cars stored by Day, Month or Season. Called for and Delivered. Also Cars for Hire with Skilled Operator in Charge.

Just in case you're curious —

$1,000.00 in 1912 is equivalent to $23,779.84 in 2014 currency.

Average yearly income in 1912 was $750.00, $17,834.88 today.

Whiskey was $3.50 a gallon and milk was $.32 a gallon.

Life expectancy was 48 years old for men and 51 years for women.

We have some
**USED
TIRES**
on hand with lots of
mileage left at very
reasonable prices.

WomenShop
Here
Real politeness, clean
surroundings, honest
prices and workman-
ship, make it attractive
for women to deal
with us.

**GOODRL 'H
No. 4
RUBBER
CEMENT** **10c**

Cover your
**SPARE TIRE
FREE**
We give you a hand-
some tire cover
with every Silver-
town purchase.

Big Reward!

for the WORST 30x3½ tire
on The Road!

Bring your car to this remarkable contest. Let
us look over your tires. To the motorist having
the worst 30x3½ tire entered in this contest, we
will give

A New
Goodrich Silvertown
FREE

All tires entered must be in use on a
car. Don't miss this opportunity to
win a new tire!

The Place: At our store

The Time: Saturday, 1 p. m. sharp

Decision made—free tire awarded, on
the spot.

Aggen & Son
726 Erie Avenue   Phone 2417-J   Sheboygan, Wis.

BEST IN Goodrich Silvertowns **THE LONG RUN**

Aladdin Soap Co.,

SHEBOYGAN, WIS.

Manufacturers of the famous

Witch Self-Washing Soap.

Try it once and you will never be without it. Save the wrappers and get some beautifully framed pictures free.

Women Made Young

Bright eyes, a clear skin and a body full of youth and health may be yours if you will keep your system in order by regularly taking

GOLD MEDAL

HAARLEM OIL

CAPSULES

The world's standard remedy for kidney, liver, bladder and uric acid troubles; the enemies of life and looks. In use since 1696. All druggists, three sizes.

Look for the name Gold Medal on every box and accept no imitation

Motorcycle Races

AT COUNTY FAIR GROUNDS, PLYMOUTH

July 4th Arranged By Sheboygan Motorcycle Club **July 4th**

☞ 10 -- Real Speed Races -- 10 ☜

Commencing at 2:30 P. M. Sharp

Best Riders in the State Are Entered

Admission 25 cents   Admission 25 cents

Our Special "20th Century"

The Beer Everybody Wants

Our "Weno" and "Hika's Pride" are also excellent brands. Have a trial case sent to your home to convince you there is none better.

Centerville Brewing Co.

Phone Sheboygan Orders to 407 White

Free Balloon Ascension
and Parachute LEAP
Into Lake Michigan
⋙ AT ⋘
LAKE VIEW
Sheboygan, July 4, 5, 6 – Every Afternoon
Fireworks and Other Amusements Each Evening.

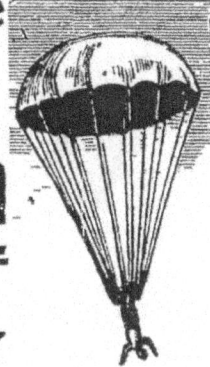

Pioneers discovered "alternate fuels" on their travels west. One prime source was buffalo chips. As the wagon trains moved across the plains, the shortage of wood for camp fires became critical, so it was soon found that buffalo chips burned fiercely, and cooked as well as wood.

These dried Buffalo chips were collected by the women and children as they walked west along the trail. There always seemed to be a steady source available. One pioneer even stated that the meat cooked over the buffalo chips needed no pepper!

The building which was recently vacated by N. E. Schils is being remodeled and will be occupied by the Kehl Cigar Company, December 1, 1909. (Kehl Cigar was located on the northeast corner of Broadway and Monroe in Sheboygan Falls.)

KEHL CIGAR COMPANY

Modern Cigarists

Get in line---our line
200 Brands to choose from

One of our many
Satisfied Customers

Weber's Delicious Chocolates, Always Fresh, Handled by Us Exclusively.

Cigar Store Indians

When Native Americans introduced tobacco to new European settlers in the wilds of 17th century America, they unwittingly became promoters of the cigar industry. Forever after, a visual picture of an Indian was often used to advertise tobacco stores.

Because of the illiteracy of the general populace, early store owners used descriptive emblems or figures to advertise their shops' wares; for example, barber poles advertised barber shops, show globes or a mortar and pestle advertised apothecaries, three gold balls represented pawn shops and an Indian signified tobacco.

While some Cigar Store Indians were made of cast iron, most were made of wood. The majority of them were made by artisans or professional carvers. Using axes, chisels, and mallets on white pine, the wooden figures were carved and then painted.

The first wooden Indians were both male and female, allowing the seller to choose which gender they wanted to help market their goods. When the wooden Indian craze first began, the female wooden Indian was used four times more often than the male wooden Indian. While female wooden Indians were occasionally carved with a papoose, and donned with a headdress of tobacco leaves instead of feathers, male figures were often dressed in the traditional warbonnets (a ceremonial headdress) of the Plains Indians.

OF CIGAR BOXES AND TOBACCO PAILS

The term recycling has become a household word in recent years, but the old cigar boxes and tobacco pails of yesteryear were put to adaptive uses long before we knew that the word meant.

In the early part of this century tobacco was considered a staple commodity in Sheboygan County households. No one had heard of the products being injurious to your health and cigars and tobacco were extensively consumed. One must remember, however, that the ladies at that time were not openly indulging in the habit and most of the users were men.

Cigarettes were just coming into their own and cigar smoking and chewing tobacco among the male population were signs of a manly stature. The smoking of a cigar or pipe was thought to give relief from stress. Lighting up a Havana was a

INDIAN FIGURES CARVED OF WOOD marked the cigar stores of years ago just as wooden horses were the trademark of harness shops. The picture above, taken in the early 1890s, shows the staff of the Trier Bros. cigar shop and the carved Indian squaw mounted on rollers so it could be moved inside at night. From left to right are: William Trier Sr., and Adolph Trier, the proprietors, their father, John Trier, who packed the cigars made in the shop, Clara Thieme, Mr. Eberhardt, Fred Burhop, William Trier Jr., Fred Kneevers and Frank Trier. At least two of the persons pictured, Fred Burhop and Fred Kneevers, are still living. Mr. Burhop later operated a cigar shop of his own and Mr. Kneevers, who now lives at 912 Pennsylvania Ave., worked for him. At the time this picture was taken the Gutsch tavern was on the corner and the Trier Bros. shop adjoined it. Note the board walk and hitching post. A sign beside the door reads "Cigars, Smoking and Chewing To-

special occasion, whereas a chew of Plow Boy or Kentucky Long Cut distended the cheeks of the users on a rather steady basis.

These vices created a lucrative market for the tobacco industry and farmers in our state joined the Southerners in the growing of tobacco. The manufacture of cigars expanded even into our area and several brand names were produced in Sheboygan County. Some of the varieties popular with the local smokers were imported from Cuba or the South. The Havana was top shelf. Dan Patch was the most eye-appealing and the Shoe Peg featured a wooden peg inserted in one end of the cigar. When the peg was removed it provided an easy draft on the business end of the cigar when lighting up. One brand, however, was strictly a local product and was manufactured in Howards Grove. Paul Janke was the cigar maker of a brand called Euneva, which derived its name from the word, avenue, spelled backwards.

Cigars were packed fifty to the box and distributed throughout the area. The box, constructed of thin wood measuring approximately nine by five and one half by two and one half inches was probably purchased from a supplier. A layer of white paper embellished the inside of the box while the outside carried the title of the brand name, the manufacturer's number and a revenue stamp.

The box of cigars was passed around at anniversary parties and at events announcing the arrival of an addition to a family. Other than that, the cigar box held a place of easy access for the man of the house for his Sunday smoke or whenever the spirit moved him.

Since the boxes were of sturdy construction, of convenient size, and were equipped with a practical cover, once the contents were consumed the cigar box became a most recyclable item. Women converted them into sewing kits, medicine chests, cosmetic cases and recipe files. Children utilized the boxes for marble storage, doll cut-outs, containers for puzzles, small wagons once wheels and axles from the Tinker Toy set were attached and even a banjo by cutting a hole in the cover and attaching strings and a strip of wood for the neck. The head of the family found the boxes handy for storing nuts and bolts, veterinary supplies, a few tools for this Model T car, and some for valuable papers and receipts.

Outside the home, the cigar box often served as a cash box at public functions. At dance halls the admission agent required two boxes — one for making change and one to contain little snips of ribbon and a pin dispensed to identify those participants who paid.

Suffice it to say that though the word "recycle" has been resurrected in recent times, many of the old-timers will agree that the old cigar boxes stand head and shoulders above other candidates.

January 21, 1905–
Sheboygan's fifteen cigar factories manufactured 1,699,115 cigars during 1904 according to re-turns made to Henry Trester, deputy collector of internal revenue. The four counties in Mr. Trester's district, Sheboygan, Ozaukee, Manitowoc and Calumet, turned out 7,893,400 cigars in 1904.

Kehl Cigar Store was located in Sheboygan Falls in 1900. A local brand produced here was named Frog.

Trier Cigar Store Indian and Employees. The cigar makers and clerks at the Trier Brothers Tobacco Shop pose with the wooden Indian. Note, too, the hitching post. Customers would tie their horses to the post while transacting business in the store.

H. C. Prange Ad
1896

H.C.PRANGE

Just opened a large line of

MISSES' and CHILDREN'S
TRIMMED HATS

6 Doz. Childs Sailor hats at 18c
Cheap at 25 cents.

6 doz. Sailor Hats at 25c
Cheap at 35 cents.

Elegently Trimmed Hats at
50, 60, 75, and 85c, $1, and $1.25.

Boys Straw Hats From 10c up.

H. C. PRANGE,
731 - - Eighth Street

—From an 1896 issue of
Sheboygan Daily Journal.

45,968 FLIES KILLED IN FIVE DAYS

May 8, 1916

The children attending fourteen schools in Sheboygan last week killed just 45,968 flies in four days, according to the reports of the teachers and principals to the civic committee of the Woman's club. The children of the Fifth Ward school led with 8,418 flies and received $7.40.

The records of the other schools show the following: First Ward, $0.08; Second Ward, $1.25; Third Ward, $2.12; Sixth Ward, $5.81; Seventh Ward, $6.84; Eighth Ward, $4.50; Washington School, $5.67; Holland School, $0.50; Holy Name School, $4.45; St. Peter Claver Catholic School, $0.60; Trinity Lutheran School, $3.33; Bethlehem Lutheran, $1.59; Immanual Lutheran, $0.80. The total amount paid out was $44.95.

January 29, 1920 Sheboygan Press

The Sheboygan Press   April 3, 1916

Black Minorca Hen Lays a Large Egg

A black Minorca hen owned by Louis Metzner, 1917 North Eleventh street, has laid an egg eight and one-half inches in periphery around the ends and six and one-half inches around the middle. Some hen that!

Egg With Three Yolks At Newton

A report comes from Manitowoc County that a white leghorn hen in Newton laid such a large egg that it attracted the attention of Mrs. Joseph A. Linsmeyer and family. When the egg was opened , the surprise of the family was heightened by the discovery that it contained three yolks.

ICE CREAM CONES TO BE MADE HERE

Nine ice cream cone machines arrived in the city yesterday. They were assigned to Walter Timm who is going to open a factory here under the name of the Sheboygan Cone Mfg Co. This will give the people of Sheboygan a chance to eat real fresh cones. The public is assured extra quality cones as Mr Timm has had six years of experience in the cone business

SATURDAY, JUNE 28.

HISTORY OF THE WORLD TWO-IN-ONE PUZZLE.

Add and subtract according to pictures, etc., and you will then be able to find out the name of the navy yard that was seized by the Confederate troops April 20, 1861   After you have done this find the picture of one of the sailors.

Answer to last puzzle. Southern Confederacy. Picture between boy and teacher

"Onyx" Hosiery

TRADE   MARK

The "Onyx" Brand will give better wear than any hosiery shown. For Men, Women and Children, from 35c. to $5.00 per pair, in any color or style you wish from Cotton to Silk.   Be sure to look for the mark shown above stamped on every pair.   Sold by all good

LORD & TAYLOR Wholesale Distributors **NEW YORK**

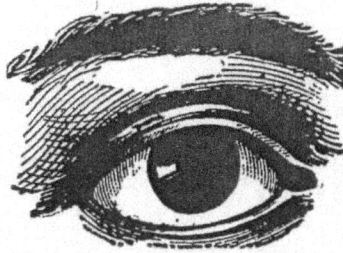

Spectacles AND Eye Glasses
$1.00

10 year guaranteed gold filled, not plated, spectacles and eye-glasses fitted with best quality, ground spherical reading lenses in frames or rimless for only $1.00.

AN INTRODUCTION OFFER

I am a new specialist here and in order to introduce myself and the class of work I do for the spectacle public I make this special offering for a few days.

I examine the eyes by the new method (the most accurate known) which does away with all kinds of machines and the old idea of having to change your glasses every once in a while.

EVERY PAIR OF THESE $1.00 GLASSES will be made to fit properly. Just the same if you paid the regular $5.00 a pair price for them as I have a reputation to protect as well as you your money.

So-Easy
The dainty eye glass, finger mounting, fitted to your lenses if you wish for only **$1.50**

Invisible Bifocal Lenses
Two in one for near and far seeing

the kind you pay $10.00 and $12.00 for regularly for only **$5.75**

Those with difficult eyes to fit or with unsatisfactory glasses will find it to their advantage to come and let me show what can be done for you. It costs you nothing for this information.

Ground lenses to order at very low prices.

EYES EXAMINED FREE

Investigate and realize your gain. Eyes examined in the evening as well as day until 9 P. M.

—SEE WINDOW DISPLAY—

Dr. C. N. Vanzant, - Eye - Specialist
AT ARTHUR F. RAAB'S, CITY NEWS DEPOT
809 N. 8th Street, Sheboygan
Here until I get a permanent location

WOOD TIRE SILO MAKES A BIG HIT

Commencing in a small way five o- six years ago and reorganizing and starting on a larger basis in January, 1914, the Wood Tire Silo Co. of Sheboygan Falls, is now doing a most satisfactory business. New buildings were erected in 1914 on Clark street the west limits of the Falls, and next to or along side of a spur track connecting directly with the main track of the C. & N. W. Railway. The factory building is 48x64 and the warehouse 22x120. The company has ample grounds for further building when necessary.

Herman L. Boldt, mayor of the Falls, is president of the company, the other officers being Julius K. Widder, vice-president and general manager and George A. Robbins, secretary and treasurer. Mr. Robbins also has charge of establishing agencies throughout Wisconsin and adjoining states.

The company has sold hundreds of their silos in Sheboygan county alone, so these silos have been thoroughly tested for several years and the owners of each are boosters for them. To verify this the company has highly complimentary testimonials from each testifying to their satisfaction. Pinehurst Farm, Sheboygan Falls has one of these Silos and their is one also at the former county home of Mr. Ernst Gonzenbach, near the Falls.

The Mohusam milk route farm at the Falls has three of them in use, and Louis Boeckmann of Lima has two. A few of the other well known farmers of the county using and recommending this silo are John P. Goelzer of Plymouth; L. Dyke, W. W. Ford and Wm. F. Craig of Waldo, Wm. Obrink and Garret Wieberdink, of Holland; Gerret TeSelle, Wilfred Humphrey, Geo. Kappleman, the Littlefields and a dozen others along the Dye road. J. H. Van Owerkirk at the Falls is another owner and booster.

It is claimed for this company's silo that it is a substantial, permanent farm building; simple of construction and easy to build; will not rack out of shape or collapse; has hollow walls and the air space keeps the silage from freezing; hollow walls being thoroughly ventilated, prevents decay of the silo; inner wall is of California Redwood which will not swell, shrink or decay, cures and keeps silage perfectly; requires no hoops or guy wires, presents an attractive appearance, made by experienced silo builders; price is reasonable and it is guaranteed for twenty years and will last a life time.

The company is doing a thriving business and is gradually branching out into the adjoining states and is one of the busy concerns that is helping to put Sheboygan Falls on the map.

The Wood Tire Silo Co. also manufactures the "Easy" Cow Stanchions which are finding a ready market.

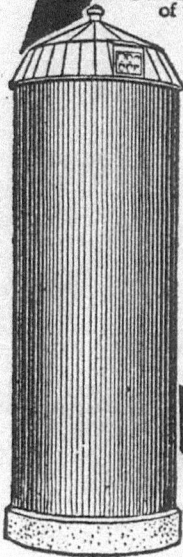

Wood Tire Hollow Wall Silo

Look at the right hand illustration and see one of the superior features of this silo, the HOLLOW WALL with the big air space in it. Positively the only practical insulation against heat, cold and moisture. This makes the ensilage keeping quality of this silo 100 per cent perfect.

Will Last a Lifetime

Guaranteed for 20 years against bursting from either the pressure of the silage or from decay, if properly erected and cared for. -=ner wall is of redwood, the wood which longest resists decay and does not swell nor shrink. Walls solidly bolted to the concrete foundation. No guy wires needed. Will not rack, sag, twist or collapse. The strong WOOD TIRES and truss-built braces between the walls prevent this.

Wood Tire
HOLLOW WALL SILO

WOOD TIRES are not bent wooden hoops. They are strong rigid trusses built up of four lateral layers of overlapping boards securely fastened together and then sawed to perfect circles at the factory.

Erect This Silo Yourself

Write us today for catalog which fully describes this superior silo and tells how you can easily and quickly erect it.

0-3

WOOD TIRE SILO CO.
Clark Street
SHEBOYGAN FALLS, WIS.
"The Silo Center of America"

WOOD
TIRE

REDWOOD
INNER
WALL

OUTER
WALL

VENTILATED
AIR
SPACE

CONCRETE
BASE

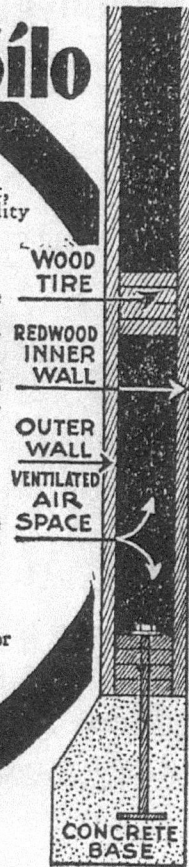

Wood Tire Silo Company. The Wood Tire Silo Company began as the Falls Stanchion Company in 1914. The company manufactured wood tire, hollow wall silos, stanchions, bushel crates, window frames and matched siding.

The factory was located on Clark Street near the railroad tracks and J.S. Richardson.

Julius Widder, George Robbins and H.E. Boldt were stockholders in the company.

These were supposed to be easily erected silos made of redwood that lasted a lifetime.

Sheboygan County to get a New Courthouse

Architect's Drawing Of The Proposed Court House Building To Be Erected On The Present Site

County Courthouse News

An impressive three-story courthouse was erected between 1866 and 1868 at Sixth Street and Center Avenue at a cost of $65,000. It featured eight chimneys to accommodate wood stoves throughout the building. A stately tower which supported a clock and huge bell used as a fire alarm. This building served the county for the next sixty-five years until 1933 when a new building of Art Deco design was erected just north and west of the old site.

The historic Seth Thomas clock of the old courthouse was reinstalled in the tower of Franklin School. The weights extend from the clockworks in the tower to the ground. It was said, people will not miss the old courthouse, but they will miss the sound of the clock as it strikes the hour and the clock in the neighborhood.

Art Deco in style, the new building is filled with marble and Indiana limestone, carvings and beautiful fixtures. It is a sight to behold and does the county proud.

Architects for the new county courthouse were W.C. Weeks, Inc. , K.M. Vitzthum &Co., and Satre & Senescall. Honold and LaPage worked on the wiring, fixtures, morgue and refrigeration. The Otto Kuechle Company supplied furniture in the ladies' rest rooms, ladies' jurors rooms, Board Committee room, jurors' dining room and the Matron's rooms.

Above: Construction of the new county courthouse begins at left in 1933 while the old one was still in use.

Below: The stately old courthouse once located at 6th and Center.

BUILDS ROOF IN HIS SLEEP

Workman Is Surprised at Wielding Hammer When Noise Attracts Others—Tacked Three Rows.

Wooster, O.—John Hoover, tinner, employed by Jacob Kauffman in Wayne county, is the prize somnambulist. The other day Kauffman was engaged in putting a roof on a barn near Reedsburg. Rain stopped him and he spent the night in the barn with his employes. They intended to finish the work in the morning.

Kauffman was awakened during the night by sounds from the roof and found Hoover at work. When Hoover came down for more tin he dropped a hammer on his foot. He rubbed his eyes and looked surprised. He had tacked on three rows of tin while asleep.

The workmanship was perfect.

SWALLOWED A PIECE OF GUM

Startled Gum-Chewer, Reproved by Court, Nearly Chokes Before He Can Explain to Judge.

Easton, Pa.—While presiding over a case in court here the other day Judge Staples of Monroe county, who is sitting in the absence of Judge Scott, took exception to the gum-chewing activities of a young man on the witness stand.

"Stop chewing that gum!" ordered the court sharply. The witness made no motion to remove the big wad that had distorted his cheek.

"Did you hear what I said? Remove that gum!" repeated the court, more sternly than before.

With flushed face and in a choking voice the witness replied: "Judge, I swallowed it!"

The court itself was forced to join in the laugh than followed.

FIRE WARNING FAR AHEAD

Pittsburgh. — (UP) — Edward Weinheimer is certain his house and barn will burn down "in a year or so". Weinheimer, who cultivates 66 acres in nearby Snowden township, based his prediction on the estimated time is will take an underground mine fire to creep to his buildings.

Sheboygan Press —

February 12, 1940

January 3, 1912

Man Ran Naked in Streets.

Trenton, N. J.—After running naked a mile through the fashionable streets of the city in broad daylight, Andrew Rosebud was captured by the police, wrapped in a horse blanket and taken to central police station, where he awaits an inquiry into his sanity

HEAD HUNTER OF NEW GUINEA

The illustration shows a young Pa puan, of Hood peninsula, British New Guinea, wearing a plume of white cockatoo feathers, which shows that he has slain an enemy in single combat. It would seem that the wearing of such plumes must soon die out Head hunting is now a forbidden joy to the Papuan. A result of this prohibition of what was a national sport throws a curious light on the effects that so called civilization may have on aborigines. The Papuan, well supplied by nature with food, had no need to work and will not work now Not so very long ago, however, he spent much time in strenuous head hunting. This kept him exercised and in good health. Now that he is not allowed to head hunt, it is said that he has begun to degenerate.

Eagle Carries Child Away
Source: Davenport Weekly Leader, Davenport, Iowa July 27, 1900

Sheboygan, Wis. July 26 - An eagle measuring six feet one and a half feet from tip to tip of wings was killed by T. Smith, a farmer living in the town of Sheboygan Falls. While at work he saw the great bird fly close to his children and clasp his daughter, Mary, aged 3 years. The man secured a rifle and shot the eagle. The child and bird fell to the ground, the child not being injured.

Sheboygan Press—January 3, 1912

Bowling in 1780.

If you bow to anyone passing by, do it in this manner: Raise the right hand to your hat gracefully.

Put your forefinger as far as the crown, and your thumb under the crim, and then raise it from your head gracefully and easily.

Look at the person you bow to, and hold your body gently forward

Hold your left arm straight down at your side, neither drawing it forward nor backward

Move the right leg, if the person goes by on the right side, and keep the other firm.

If the person goes by on the left side, move the left leg, and keep the right firm.

Let your body be bowed moderately, not too much.—November Atlantic

Sheboygan Press — Leo, a black Nubian lion, was the living trademark of Metro Goldwyn Mayer Pictures. He was insured for $1,000,000 and was purported to be the heaviest and longest lion in captivity. On Monday, July 22, 1929 he stopped in Sheboygan as part of a five- year promotional world tour which designed to promote the movie studio. Leo traveled from stop to stop in his cage that was mounted on an REO Speedwagon truck.

At the Sheboygan Press, a photographer entered the 24 foot cage to take his picture. At the Sheboygan Theater he performed stunts for the audience, including kneeling and saying his prayers. Leo split his usual rations of 25 pounds of meat a day into meals at Joe Bensman's Meat Market, Diamond Meat Market, and The Sanitary Cash Meat Market. In an interview with the Sheboygan Press, Leo's trainer, Captain Volney Phifer, said that he had come from a long line of animal trainers, going back at least four generations on both sides of his family.

MGM had trademarked Leo's very distinctive roar which appeared at the beginning of their films for decades. Leo seemingly was a cat with nine lives: while touring the globe for MGM, he survived two train wrecks, a Mississippi flood, a California earthquake, a fire and a plane crash. He died at an advanced age of 23, in 1938, and is buried in Gillette, New Jersey, on the farm owned by Volney Phifer, premier animal trainer.

Above: Greta Garbo with Leo on the MGM Promotional World Tour.

Taken from the Sheboygan Press, January 6, 1936

A terrific explosion at 9 p.m. Saturday blew to smithereens another remnant of the good old horse and buggy days. It was one of this nation's last few. Most of them are gone, but they and their purpose have been immortalized in that unusual essay, "The Specialist," by Charles (Chic) Sale.

Whether it was a two-holer or a three-holer could not be determined because where it once stood at 1816 North Tenth Street, only a pile of kindling wood remains.

An improvised heating system installed by its user, Alfred Smith caused the explosion. The tiny, one story, frame structure had out-lived its usefulness and been converted into a repair shop.

The fire department estimated the damage to the structure itself at $25 and damage to the contents at $50. The loss in dollars does not matter. The loss as a landmark, as a historical building, as a building significant to the days when America was a young and struggling nation, cannot be estimated.

Chic Sale's humorous monologue was about a carpenter who built outhouses. Chic Sale was an actor. Starting in vaudeville, he appeared on the legitimate stage, and then in films in the early days of Hollywood. As a member of Rotary, he would attend meetings in the cities where he was performing. He was often asked to provide some "little" entertainment after the luncheons. Since many of his routines required elaborate props, he chose to do a short monologue, written for the occasion. It was a comedy piece about Lem Putt, country carpenter and specialist in building out-

FREE HAM
Given to the Fattest Man
attending the
**AIRPORT TAVERN
TONIGHT**
Good Music—5c Beer
Free Warm Lunch

115

Poem By Local Girl Brings Letter From White House

Helen Mae de Geus, 13, 1613 N. Fouth street, has received a letter from M. A. Le Hand, private secretary to President Franklin D. Roosevelt, thanking her for the poem which she wrote and dedicated to the latter on his fifty-third birthday which is today.

The letter said, "The president has been especially pleased to receive your poem of birthday greetings and asks me to tell you that he greatly appreciates your kind thought."

The poem which Helen wrote and which was accompanied by a note expressing her "sincerest wishes for a happy birthday and many more" follows:

To Our President On His Birthday

To you, our own brave president,
We raise our voice in praise,
And join in wishing you,
Many more birthdays.

You've steered us through the years,
You've led us through the days,
And now in happy greeting,
Our voices we will raise.

Health to you, our Captain,
You have helped us through,
The bravest man who ever lived,
Happy birthday to you.

January 30, 1935

Sheboygan Press
April 2, 1928

PENNILESS MAN RETURNS PURSE HE FOUND TO OWNER

Racine, Wis. — (AP) — Diogenes should have lighted his lamp in Racine to achieve success at finding an honest man.

John Armstrong, 31, homeless and penniless, sought shelter at the police station.

"One block west and a half block north," police told him he would find "the tramp house" which afforded hospitality to such as he.

On the way over Armstrong found a purse which he returned unopened to the police. The thirty dollars which it contained was claimed by Ole Breeland.

Comfort Indoor Closet

A Scientific Solution of a Perplexing Problem
Odorless---Sanitary---Germ Proof

A modern convenience for rural and village homes. Gives comfort and convenience. Saves time and health. Eliminates the unsightly, badsmelling disease breeding outhouse.

COMFORT HAPPINESS HEALTH
The Comfort Indoor Closet brings joy and health to the entire family. It is the lowest priced health preserver known. Thousands are using them in America. It is the most modern convenience that has been given to the thousands of people who live where running water and sewerage are not obtainable. It gives greater convenience than the city flush closet and at a much less cost. It is cheaper to buy and install than than it is to build the most ordinary outside closet. Are you going to continue using a cold, inconvenient, unhealthy, disease breeding outside closet!

Comfort Indoor Closet is Complete
Everything you need is furnished complete with the closet and at the price. It is equipped to set up and connect with the chimney. If you want to use it away from the chimney, then you can order the needed parts from the "extra parts list" at a very small additional cost and they will be shipped with the Comfort Closet. The following is a complete list of parts showing the standard equipment. These are enamelized and the same finish as closet--Closet (outer casing), galvanized steel container, mahoganized closet seat, all metal lid with rubber protector, eight feet of vent pipe, lower elbow, upper elbow, reducer, wall collar, one gallon Comfort chemical, roll of toilet paper, toilet paper holder. Our special large size $18.50, Standard size $14.50. F. O. B. Milwaukee.

For further particular and to see closet call on
W. J. SULLIVAN, Campbellsport, Wis

J. F. WALSH   J. P. VAN BLARCUM

Comfort Indoor Closet

A Scientific Solution of a Perplexing Problem
Oderless---Sanitary---Germ Proof.

A modern convenience (for rural and village homes. Gives comfort and convenience. Saves time and health. Eliminates the unsightly, badsmelling disease breeding outhouse.

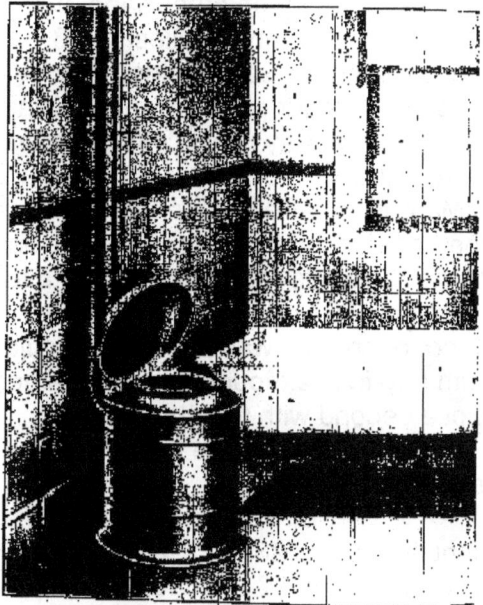

COMFORT HAPPINESS HEALTH
The Comfort Indoor Chemical Closet brings joy and health to the entire family. It is the lowest priced health preserver known. Thousands are using them in America. It is the most modern convenience that has been given to the thousands of people who live where running water and sewerage are not obtainable. It gives greater convenience than the city flush closet and at a much less cost. It is cheaper to buy and install than than it is to build the most ordinary outside closet. Are you going to continue using a cold, inconvenient, unhealthy, disease breeding outside closet!

117

STORK HAS BUSY YEAR
VISITS OVER 1,100 FAMILIES IN
THE COUNTY DURING PAST ELEV-
EN MONTHS

Births far exceed deaths in the county according to the vital statistics given out by the register of deeds this week relating to the eleven months so far this year.

There were 668 deaths in the county during the eleven months, the largest occuring in January, when eighty-eight persons answered the summons of the grim reaper. On the other hand, the stork visited county families 1,143 times during the same period, the greatest number of visits being during the month of May, when 135 children were born.

Marriages were unable to keep up the pace set by the other two divisions of the register's record book, and a total of only 397 unions was reported. June, of course, was the most popular with fifty-five, although October came a close second with fifty-three.

The following are the figures for the eleven months:

	Births	Marriages	Deaths
January	128	20	88
February	87	31	61
March	89	28	60
April	111	14	53
May	135	42	63
June	101	55	63
July	94	23	60
August	115	24	41
September	117	52	77
October	89	53	45
November	67	45	47
Totals	1143	397	668

The figures for the month of November, just completed by the register, compare as follows with last year: 1915, Births 67; marriages, 58; deaths, 38.

STORK HAS
A BUSY YEAR

VISITS OVER 1,100 FAMILIES IN
THE COUNTY DURING PAST
ELEVEN MONTHS

Births far exceed deaths in the county according to the vital statistics given out by the register of deeds this week relating to the eleven months so far this year.

There were 668 deaths in the county during the eleven months, the largest occuring in January, when eighty-eight persons answered the summons of the grim reaper. On the other hand, the stork visited county families 1,143 times during the same period, the greatest number of visits being during the month of May, when 135 children were born.

Marriages were unable to keep up the pace set by the other two divisions of the register's record book, and a total of only 397 unions was reported. June, of course, was the most popular with fifty-five, although October came a close second with fifty-three.

The following are the figures for the eleven months:

	Births	Marriages	Deaths
January	128	20	88
February	87	31	61
March	89	28	60
April	111	14	53
May	135	42	63
June	101	55	63
July	94	23	60
August	115	24	41
September	117	52	77
October	89	53	45
November	67	45	47
Totals	1143	397	668

The figures for the month of November, just compiled by the register, compare as follows with last year: 1915, Births 67; marriages, 58; deaths, 38.

DEATH AND BURIAL TRADITIONS

'Corpse' Enjoys His Funeral

Pleased as pie, bewhiskered Felix "Bush" Breazeale fans himself in front of the coffin, which he built himself, and enjoys the eulogy as a minister preaches his "funeral." Bush ordered the ceremonies held at a little church in Kingston, Tenn., on his 74th birthday so there would be "no question of a preacher gettin' things wrong" about him after his death. More than 12,000 people gathered for the occasion.

From a marker
in Enosburg Falls, Vermont

Here lies the body of our dead Anna,
Gone to death by a banana.
It wasn't the fruit that dealt the blow,
But the skin of the thing that laid her low.

****

In a Thurmont, Maryland
cemetery

Here lies an Atheist
All dressed up
And no place to go.

Here lies John Auricular,
Who in the ways of the Lord
walked perpendicular.

New York Times – September 20, 1860

Among the victims of the *Lady Elgin* calamity was Mr. Wm. Farnsworth, of Sheboygan, Wis. His body was recovered and taken to that town, where it was buried on the Wednesday succeeding the disaster. Mr. Farnsworth was among the earliest settlers of Sheboygan. In 1818 he resided there for a few months as a trapper and Indian trader, and in 1835 returned to the town, at that time becoming proprietor of a half interest in the village plat. When speculation in lands was at its highest pitch, he sold two-sixteenths of this interest for $55,000, on for $30,000 to the New York and Erie Transportation Company, and the other to another party for $25,000. With the exception of a three or four year residence at Milwaukee, he has lived at Sheboygan since 1835.

Kick by A Dead Horse
Puts Man In The Hospital

Plymouth. - Paradoxical as it may seem, Walter Brickner was confined to the hospital here today as the result of being kicked by a dead horse. Brickner, an employee of the Edward W. Bohnsack Company at their rendering plant outside the city limits, was watching two workmen remove the carcass of a horse. One of the hind legs swing around suddenly, hitting him in the head and rendering him unconscious. Although he is suffering slight injuries to the head, his condition is not serious.

Sheboygan Press 19 Aug 1930

Mortuary Mention

Fond du Lac Journal, December 31, 1846

Sheboygan—The hand of Providence has suddenly visited this place in a singular and distressing manner, which has spread a deep gloom over the village, Mrs. Charlotte Moore, wife of J.L. Moor Esq., died on the 20th of December after an illness of about three months.

———————

September 1, 1849: Death of Gay W. Lee, Esquire.

It is with unfeigned sorrow that we announce the decease, on Sunday evening last of our esteemed townsman Gay W. Lee. Notwithstanding he had been laboring under an indisposition, a kind of chronic diarrhea, for some time previous to his death, which had not however prevented him from following his usual avocations until Wednesday last week. It cast a universal gloom over the mental horizon of our town.

———————

Taken in Youth's Sweet Spring

Miss Gertie Westerbeke Passes Away After a Long Illness

It is often said death is no respecter of persons, and it is just as true that it is often choice of those it claims. Neither is death ever a pleasant visitant, but when it takes a from her friends a favorite, a young lady who has just bloomed into young and beautiful womanhood, one whose loveliness of person and character made her beloved by all, it is too terrible for words to adequately describe.

———————

P.S. 2008

. . He was preceded in death by his parents and a brother, Donald. P.S. Whoever edits this bio can delete any or all of it, except for the part about his loving wife, Nancy.

———————

Miss Emma Buck Centenarian Dies At Home

Emma B., who ran a pre-Civil War family farm in Illinois that remained virtually unchanged into the 21st century, died on June 5 on the sleigh bed with handmade ticking she had slept in for 98 years, in the log cabin built by her great-uncle, a German immigrant, in 1849.

She was 100 or 101. Miss Buck, who had pulled the last of her own teeth some years ago, lived there without running water, drawing her water from a well. Until two days before she died, she walked to the outhouse, one of many structures on the farm.

Wisconsin's Only Escalator

The summer of 1937 witnessed the opening of Prange's new escalator . . . The only moving stairway, as it was called at the time, in Wisconsin. Prange's escalator preceded those in Milwaukee by five years. The escalator took shoppers from the first floor to the second floor, but not back down.

The escalator was electrically driven, running continuously and silently, and was capable of carrying as many as 6,000 people per hour. Situated at the rear of the store the escalator ran from the first to second floors and could accommodate as many as 42 people at one time.

Escalator Background—The earliest working type of escalator, patented in 1892 by Jesse W. Reno, was introduced as a new novelty ride at the Old Iron Pier at Coney Island NY, in 1896. But, it took the Otis Elevator Company of New York to manufacture it and get it ready for general use. It was exhibited in 1900 at the Paris Exposition, where the name "escalator" was adopted.

Potpourri

In the September 3, 1918 Sheboygan Press, there was a public notice that because of the war effort, sugar usage was limited and people needed to get canning permits.

❄

Combing sage tea into your hair transforms it from gray to your natural color.

❄

On Labor Day, 1918, Mrs. Narrowly escaped drowning when the boat she was in sprang a leak.

❄

In ads in the September 5, 1918 Sheboygan Press, the Black Cat Textile Company and Muh's Bakery were looking only for married men to fix knitting machines and deliver bread, respectively.

❄

C. A. Schreffler announced on Christmas Eve, 1918, that he was closing his women's clothing store after being in business for nine and a half years.

❄

On May 2, 1925, Otto Westphal, Gustav Thiry, and Paul Kolbe were sentenced to a year in Waupun for stealing shoes, socks, and ties from Henry Dekarske's store.

❄

Earl Nelson died on May 16, 1925, when his car left the road. He was swerving to miss some ducks crossing the road.

❄

On May 16, 1925, Miss Margaret Kamens, named "The Perfect Woman" in a New York physical culture contest, demonstrated exercises on the fourth floor of the H.C. Prange store.

❄

In 1925, merchants throughout Sheboygan declared May 29th the start of the straw hat season.

❄

 On June 18, 1900, Sheboygan smokers were warned that if they were planning to attend the Paris Exposition, that smoking was not allowed on the grounds.

❄

In 1925, John J Theune operated the Chick Store whose only merchandise was chickens.

❀

On April 19th and 20th, 1925, the Ford Hopkins Drug Store was having an Easter toiletry sale. Two thousand live baby chicks were brought in for the event.

❀

After Miss Harriet Keach of Greenbush had passed, $10,000 was found in her house. It had been hidden in books, magazines, mattresses, and even sewn in-to furniture upholstery.

❀

Standing 8'7" and weighing 450 pounds, Cliff Thompson, of Scandavia, Wisconsin was the biggest man in the world at that time. On January 27,1938, he visit-ed the Manitowoc Rotary club at their meeting.

❀

Hinze's sold licorice-flavored black ice cream for the Fourth of July, 1940. Skinless wieners were more expensive than veal chops, rose fish, and pork roast at the A&P store in 1940.

According to an H.C. Prange ad in the December 24, 1947 Sheboygan Press, a shopper could buy an entire chicken in a can for $2.19

❀

In August of 1957, you could get a low calorie lunch of three Jello cubes, fresh fruit, and cottage cheese for 50 cents at Kresge's.

❀

On August 1, 1957, both a 15 year old and a 16 year old boy stole a case of beer off the Kingsbury loading dock.

❀

On August 2, 1957, a single swim fin was found on Superior Avenue between twelfth and thirteenth streets.

❀

Cleobratra was the winning entry in the "Name The Pig" contest at the 1957 Bratwurst Days. The winner was Maurice Monahan from Dacada.

According to a story in the January 2, 1951 Sheboygan Press, a surgeon performed an operation with tin shears on New Year's Day at St. Mary's Hospital in Grand Rapids, Michigan.

On Tuesday, January 30, 1951, on a wrestling card at the Playdium, midgets Tom Thumb and Pee Wee James grappled in a hard fought match. Billy Goelz and Gypsy Joe battled in the main event.

P.T. Barnum and Tom Thumb.

Sheboygan Smokers "Reached For Cigarettes" — 30 Million Smoked Here During 1928

How many cigarettes were smoked in Sheboygan, Wisconsin, during 1928?

From the statistics just issued by the Internal Revenue bureau, many interesting things can be figured out.

For instance:

In the United States, during the last year, 105,915,165,014 cigarettes were smoked —at least they were bought, as the tax returns show. Now, the estimated population of the country is 120,013,-000. Of hat number 35,000 live here in Sheboygan. Dividing 120,013,000 by 35,000 gives 3,429. Then all one has to do to discover how many cigarettes have been smoked here in Sheboygan is to divide 105,915,165,014 by 3,429. The result is 30,888,062 were smoked in 1928 here in Sheboygan.

Perhaps Sheboygan went a little over its quota or a little under, but that is the number which should have been smoked here if it did its exact share in the cigarette consumption of the year.

That the use of cigarettes has grown amazingly is shown by these figures. In 1927 which had been looked upon as a banner year, 97,176,607,481 cigarettes were sold. That means that the increase for 1928 was 8,739,357,-530. If that number is divided by the percentage of Sheboygan's population to that of the United States, it will be seen that more cigarettes were smoked here in 1928 than in the preceding year, always supposing that Sheboygan

Peter Dinkel (1850-1924) was an enterprising and interesting man. Dinkel was a painter, a bartender and a saloon keeper, a restauranteur, a well-known bird naturalist and a merchant. He was the first to sell Edison and Victor phonographs and phonograph records. Besides "talking machines," his business establishments on Pennsylvania Avenue and later on Eighth Street, also sold music boxes, cigars, wines and liquors, and a variety of imported birds—primarily canaries—that sang.

Badger State Bird Store
PETER DINKEL
Importer of and Dealer in
First - Class Canary
and other Birds
Also Bird Food of best Quality
511 N. 8. St.   Sheboygan, Wis.
The best Equipped Store of its kind
"Victor" Talking Machines, and records

PETER DINKEL,
Breeder and Importer of
..FINE..
Singing Birds
of all kinds.
..A Selected Stock Always on Hand..
Also Dealer in Bird Seeds.
434 PENNSYLVANIA AVE.
N. W. TELEPHONE 216.
SHEBOYGAN, : WIS.
2

Chillicothe Morning Constitution - Chillicothe, Missouri - July 28, 1906

The Farm Floated Away

Sheboygan, Wis, July 27 - The mysterious disappearance of a thirty-seven acre farm on the shore of Long Lake in Fond du Lac county was cleared today by the discovery that the tract had worked loose and drifted into the lake as floating bog.

Weekly Sentinel - Ft. Wayne, Indiana - February 21, 1906

First Bath In Fifty Years

Sheriff Forces Sheboygan, Wis., Man to Break Old Vow

Sheboygan, Wis., Feb. 15 - Nicholas Hoffman, who is 64 years old, bathed today for the first time in fifty years. He made a vow when he was 14 years old that he would never take another bath. A sheriff, who stood by the bath tub while Hoffman bathed today forced him to break his vow.

Oakland Tribune - Oakland California - September 8, 1904

Sheriff Amuses Babies; Prisoners Escape

Three Burglars and a Forger Get Out of Jail
While Proud Father Plays With Twins

Chicago, September 8 - A dispatch to the Tribune from Sheboygan, Wis., says: Four prisoners, one a forger and three burglars, have sawed their way out of the Sheboygan County Jail while the Sheriff was playing with his twin babies in an adjoining office.

All are supposed to have escaped from the city on a freight train.

Daily Iowa State Press - Iowa - October 25, 1901

Asks $3,000 for Her Kisses

A circuit court jury at Sheboygan, Wis., awarded Mrs. Bouska, of the town of Adell, a verdict for $500 as balm. Peter Nugent was the defendant in the case. He promised Mrs. Bouska one dollar for every kiss she gave him. Failing to collect she instituted suit. She asked the court for $3,000 damages..

Haunted House

On May 3, 1894, John Schwartz sold a piece of property on the northern most point of Turtle Bay to Julius G. Wagner of Milwaukee. On that property there was an abandoned house which had been unoccupied for years and eventually acquired a reputation as being, "Haunted." Who or when the house was built isn't known and only one picture of it exists, probably taken about the time it was torn down. All that is known about it is the following article from the Plymouth Reporter of August 30, 1894.

"Elkhart Lake is about to lose one of its greatest attractions, the haunted house. Not that it is so beautiful in itself, but because of that element of romance and that smack of the supernatural, which have hung about it."

… The old gray walls with their staring windows are quite gloomy enough for the gruesome tale attached to them. The story goes that a man was murdered there long ago, and each night at the mystic hour of twelve, his spirit revisits the spot. A maple tree with foliage of a peculiar, sickly shade of greenish-yellow unlike any other near the lake stands near the house. The tree was a normal color until the night of the murder.

As might be expected the house is a favorite haunt of young people. Many a midnight party has been formed to investigate this interesting phantom. Nothing has ever been found but the ghost remains a fascinating mystery.

This is the only known image of the house taken from a lantern slide. Who is that ghostly image of the lady in gray?

According to a Sheboygan Press article, Harvey Hinze, the former manager of the Grand Candy Kitchen, went into business for himself in 1932. Starting at 1220 Michigan Avenue, he later moved to his more familiar location at 920 Michigan Avenue. He made over forty types of candies, including fudge, brittles, and creams. A specialty was malt crunch candy. He made over 150 flavors of ice cream from licorice to Cantaloupe. Hinze was known for sundaes such as Duke's Delight, Pig's Dinner, and the Big Shot. Besides the shop on Michigan Avenue, also owned the Twin Whip Drive-In at Seventeenth and Erie. From 1969 to 1987, he also operated the concession stand at the Quarry.

+ Sheboygan Postmaster, Louis J. Albrecht, stated on December 23, 1947 that that year was their busiest ever. They handled 1,238,231 pieces of mail in the first 22 days of December and hired 102 temporary employees to help out. In 1946 they had only hired 68.

+ Tuesday, December 23, 1947 was the twelfth meatless Tuesday under President Truman's Food Conservation Program.

+ On January 24, 1951, six disorderly houses were raided in Sheboygan county and 26 women were arrested for soliciting.

Huge Crowd Attends "Hatching" of Easter Egg   **March 5, 1948**

Picture standing on the raised platform at the H.C. Prange Co. store on Wisconsin Avenue is the Easter bunny which just a few moments before had hatched from the huge egg seen in the background. With the bunny are Percy Rademacher, favorite clown of Sheboygan children and Hal O'Halloran of WHBL.

Sheboygan Couple Enjoys A Visit With The Former Kaiser

After an enjoyable tour of Europe, the highlight of which was a pleasant visit with former Kaiser Wilhelm von Hohenzollern and the Kaiserin, Mr. and Mrs. Otto Jung returned to their home at 318 St. Clair avenue Sunday afternoon.

The meeting with the former German emperor at Doorn, Holland, was more in the nature of an informal social visit than a formal audience. Mr. Jung having spent about a half hour discussing various topics with the former Kaiser while the Kaiserin entertained Mrs. Jung in the private gardens. Mr. Jung and the former emperor engaged in both English and German conversation. Later, after the interview, and visit the Kaiserin rejoined Mrs. Jung and helped her select some souvenir linens to be brought back to this country. Before leaving the Sheboygan couple, the former Kaiser presented both with an autographed picture of himself.

Mr. Jung says that the former Kaiser is well preserved in spite of his seventy-two years of age and appears to be in the best of health. He also speaks an excellent English. Exceptionally well versed in conditions in the United States, the former Kaiser discussed the works of some of our writers and in talking about localities immediately connected Sheboygan with Milwaukee as to proximity.

Some difficulty was encountered at first in gaining the audience with the former Kaiser. Both the man at the gateway to the state and the guide informed Mr. Jung that it was unprecedented to grant an interview without several days' notice and that furthermore it was late in the day—about four o'clock. His Majesty, said the attendant, did everything on schedule and it would be difficult to interrupt that routine. After Mr. Jung talked German, presented his papers and said that he would be in Doorn that afternoon only, he was told to return in a short time and that in the meantime his request would be taken up with the former emperor.

Upon returning Mr. and Mrs. Jung were met by the former Kaiser's aide de camp who led them through the estate in the direction of the palace. Mr. Jung thought he was being taken to the palace for a brief and formal introduction but instead he and Mrs. Jung encountered the former Kaiser in the grounds and learned that he had decided to greet them informally. The visit with the former Kaiser was about a half hour in duration.

In addition to this unusual privilege of meeting so important a character in the history of the world, Mr. and Mrs. Jung enjoyed a pleasant time throughout their journey. They only encountered one day of rain, and they report excellent accommodations at all points visited.

They left here in the middle of April and during the course of their journey visited the following places: Naples, Rome, Florence, Cernobbio and Genoa, Italy; Nice and Paris, France; London, England; Brussels, Belgium; The Hague, Netherlands; Amsterdam and Doorn, Holland; Cologne, Wiesbaden, Heidelberg, Baden Baden, Munich, Eisenach and Berlin, German; Interlaken, Lugano and Lucerne, Switzerland; Vienna, Austria.

While at Vienna, Mr. Jung attended the convention of Rotary International as a representative of the Sheboygan club. He also had been appointed one of the assistant sergeant-at-arms and served in that capacity throughout the convention.

Much privation is being suffered by people who before the war were in good financial condition in Europe, and this is particularly true in Austria and Germany, Mr. Jung says, and hopes that some way will be found as soon as possible to relieve the tense situation existing in all Europe.

Scramble For Front Rank In Contest With Heavy Voting

Candidates Bunched At Head Of Column, With Many Surprises Taking Place Today

The Sheboygan Press Popularity Contest definitely established itself as the greatest event of its kind ever conducted in this city when 182,000 new votes were counted this morning, well distributed among twenty-six active candidates who are competing for a free trip to Bermuda as "Miss Sheboygan."

Many changes took place today in the standings of the contestants, but Miss Ann Falle still holds the lead with 32,300 votes. Although in a dangerous position Friday when she was only 400 votes ahead of Miss Mary Juntz, she rallied successfully over the week-end and now has a somewhat better margin. Nevertheless, she has five other brilliant workers right at her heels, any one of whom may dislodge her by the time tomorrow's tabulations are made.

Miss Zelda Oetking swept through the ranks today, advancing from sixth place to second, pushing aside, for the time being, four of her opponents who had left her far behind last Friday. Miss Oetking's total today is 29,300, compared with 5,100 in the previous report.

The greatest surprise of the day, however, was the spectacular rise of Miss Madeline Reichert from eighteenth place to third highest, increasing her vote from a mere 400 to 28,700.

Other substantial gains were made by young women who have been steadily piling up their totals. Miss Luella Lemkuil soared from 13,400 to 28,100 for fourth place, and Miss Mary Juntz almost doubled her count from 15,300 to 28,000 for fifth place.

Miss Catherine Lamb jumped into the middle of the fray with a new total of 24,100 for sixth place. Miss Marguerite Wolf is next with 18,700, a splendid gain over her previous total of 2,800. Then follow Miss Irene M. Biwerse with 15,100, Miss Irmgard Vollbrecht with 14,600, Miss Eleanor Krueger with 13,500, and Miss Verona Molitor with 10,600.

Miss Frieda Hillmann added nine hundred votes for a total of 3,800, while Miss Helen Pfister's count took a sharp upward turn from 200 to 3,400. Miss Verona Eckardt follows with 2,900, Miss Ermalinde Birkle and Miss Lois Czamanske advanced to 1,100 and 1,000, respectively.

Six more new contestants were enrolled today, one of them, Miss Betty Gollhardt, opening with 2,500 votes, and Miss Arlisle Sperb with 1,800. The other nominees were Miss Theresa Gottsacker, Miss Irmgard Daehn, and Miss Dorothy Eichstaedt.

Thus the second week of the great contest opens with votes so evenly divided that it still is "anybody's race." At the present rate of balloting, the totals of the leaders should run into the hundreds of thousands when the final tabulation is made on July 25, the closing day of the contest.

Free votes are being given by the following merchants with cash purchases or payments on account, 100 votes with each dollar of business:

Matthewsons', Chas. A. Henold company, G. N. G. Hardware and Heating company, Fox theatre, F. Geele Hardware company, Christoph's Brown-bilt Shoe store, Charley's Fruit Market, C. Reiss Coal company (household deliveries and collections only), Fashion Shop, Sheboygan Sporting Goods company, Wagner's Meat Markets, Rose Shop, Wolf's Central Laundry, Stern's Credit store, Sheboygan theatre, Sheboygan Dry Goods company, Roenitz Drug company, W. A. Pfister Jewelry store, People's Clothing company, Kinney's Shoe store, Sheboygan Coal company, A. W. Ramm, Inc., J. G. Grandlic, Jr., Dennis Furniture company.

Be sure to ask for your votes when you do business with these merchants. You may vote for yourself, if you are a candidate, or you may vote for a friend. New nominations are welcome at any time.

Remember that it is easy to add thousands of votes to the total of any contestant. A one dollar purchase yields 100 votes, a five-dollar purchase 500 votes, a ten-dollar purchase 1,000 votes, and so on.

Standings In Popularity Contest

Names of Contestants	Votes
Miss Ann Falle, 1420 N. 17th St.	32,300
Miss Zelda Oetking, 1922 N. 4th St.	29,300
Miss Madeline Reichert, Hotel Foeste	28,700
Miss Luella Lemkuil, 1018 Los Angeles Ave.	28,100
Miss Mary Juntz, 718 Niagara Ave.	28,000
Miss Catherine Lamb, 919 N. 6th St.	24,100
Miss Marguerite Wolf, 526 Michigan Ave.	18,700
Miss Irene M. Biwerse, 1810 N. 4th St.	15,100
Miss Irmgard Vollbrecht, 823 Spring Ave.	14,600
Miss Eleanor Krueger, 1240 Lincoln Ave.	13,500
Miss Verona Molitor, 1218 Clara Ave.	10,600
Miss Bernadine Reiter, 1603 N. 7th St.	6,200
Miss Frieda Hillmann, 1529 N. 3rd St.	3,800
Miss Helen Pfister, 528 N. 9th St.	3,400
Miss Alma Schramm, 1327 N. 15th St.	3,300
Miss Verona Eckardt, 910 N. 4th St.	2,900
Miss Betty Gollhardt, 1630 S. 11th St.	2,500
Miss Arlisle Sperb, 520 N. Water St.	1,800
Miss Valeska Hinze, 1218 S. 15th St.	1,500
Miss Ermalinde Birkle, 1803 N. 20th St.	1,100
Miss Lois Czamanske, 528 Ontario Ave.	1,000
Miss Theresa Gottsacker, 1515 N. 8th St.	500
Miss Irmgard Daehn, 1124 Broadway Ave.	200
Miss Dorothy Eichstaedt, 409 Superior Ave.	200
Miss Laura Marie Bau, 1029 N. 4th St.	100
Miss Marie Verhage, 1006 Clara Ave.	100

July 6, 1931

Popularity Contest Winners

1. Miss Mary Juntz 4,916,000
   "Miss Sheboygan" —
   Free Trip to Bermuda

2. Miss Ann Falle 1,945,600
   Free Trip to Bermuda

3. Miss Lucille Kampmann 1,717,300
   Diamond Ring

4. Miss Helen Baumert 1,277,400
   Wrist Watch

5. Miss Catherine Lamb 1,003,400
   Diamond Pendant

6. Miss Madeline Reichert 927,900
   Twenty Dollars in Cash

7. Miss Zelda Oetking 912,700
   Twenty Dollars in Cash

8. Miss Marguerite Wolf 849,300
   Ten Dollars in Cash

9. Miss Irene M. Biwerse 681,100
   Ten Dollars in Cash

10. Miss Bernadine Reiter 628,200
    Ten Dollars in Cash

11. Miss Betty Gollhardt 568,000
    Ten Dollars in Cash

12. Miss Irmgard Vollbrecht 481,600
    Ten Dollars in Cash

13. Miss Verona Molitor 409,500
    Ten Dollars in Cash

14. Miss Luella Lemkuil 389,300
    Ten Dollars in Cash

(Detailed contest news and pictures on page three).

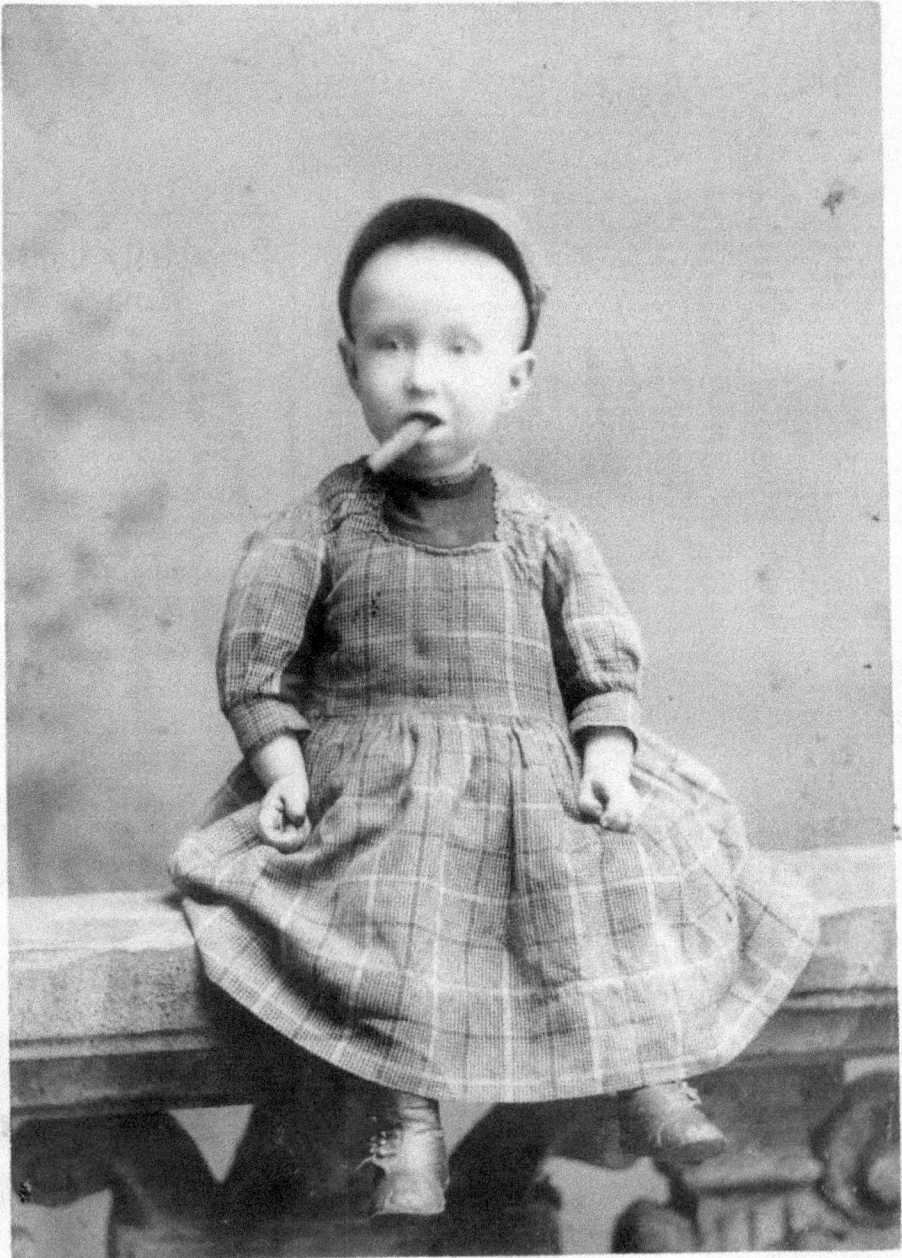

Sattler
SUMMER RESORT STUDIO
Elkhart Lake, Wis.

The End

www.ingramcontent.com/pod-product-compliance
Lightning Source LLC
Chambersburg PA
CBHW050905100426
42737CB00048B/3087